FOX-HUNTING
RECOLLECTIONS

BY

SIR REGINALD GRAHAM, BART.

SECOND IMPRESSION

Copyright © 2013 Read Books Ltd.
This book is copyright and may not be
reproduced or copied in any way without
the express permission of the publisher in writing

British Library Cataloguing-in-Publication Data
A catalogue record for this book is available from the
British Library

A Brief Introduction to Fox Hunting

In the fourteenth century and for at least two or three centuries later, foxes were but vermin, and were treated as such. Nets and greyhounds were used to capture and kill them and although early records show that our Kings were involved, we hear nothing of their having personally participated in the sport of foxhunting. They seem to have sent their huntsmen with nets and greyhounds all over the country to kill foxes for the value of the pelt as well as to relieve country folk of a thievish neighbour.

Sir T. Cockaine wrote in his treatise of 1591 of the great woodlands that once covered England which had now, for the greater part disappeared. It would seem that even in these times, foxes were becoming scarcer. Another chronicler of those times states, 'of foxes we have some, but no great store and these are rather preserved by gentlemen to hunt and have pastime withall at their own pleasure than otherwise suffered to live.' By the seventeenth century foxhunting was well established, and Blome (1686), who gives us a good account of hunting the fox 'above ground' claimed that 'of late years the knowledge of this is arrived to far greater perfection, being now become a very healthful recreation to such as delight therin.' Clearly, fox hunting was a very popular and well-respected pastime.

'Foxhunting', wrote Beckford in 1787, 'is now become the amusement of *gentlemen*: nor need any gentleman be ashamed of it.' Opinions have changed substantially since these times however, and the sport was banned in the United Kingdom in 2004. Despite this, more than two hundred packs of foxhounds are still thriving in the UK and are recruiting newcomers to the mounted field in ever increasing numbers. Most claim to just follow scent trails as opposed to actual foxes. A reasonable estimate that some two hundred and fifty thousand people in the British Isles hunt regularly with this figure swollen to over a million by those who hunt and follow intermittently during the season.

The sport of fox hunting today is probably far faster and more exciting than it used to be. In the 'golden days' of foxhunting between 1815 and 1880 most hunts consisted of the local squires and their friends, with a few farmers, doctors, parsons and professional men. Today the packs are much better organised and the field will consist of those who hunt in order to ride and those who really care to partake of the science of hunting and hound work. Unlike shooting and fishing which financially benefit large numbers of riparian owners and landowners through the lease or syndication of sporting rights, foxhunting does not pay rentals for the right to hunt over privately owned land and estates. This takes place through the goodwill of landowners who see the hunt as beneficial to the countryside by helping reduce the numbers of foxes and also for the benefits bestowed on the community by the very active social life revolving around most aspects of the hunt. The Hunt Ball, skittle and quiz evenings, open days and barn dances, all play their part in bringing both town and country together as well as raising funds to assist with the day to day running expenses incurred by a modern pack of hounds.

The publishers wish to make clear that in no way do they condone fox hunting proper. This book has been reprinted solely for its historical value and content, including practical information on horses and hounds, breeding and rearing, that is still relevant today.

CONTENTS

CHAP.		PAGE
I.	EARLY DAYS	1
II.	THE BEAUFORT HUNT	11
III.	THE BURTON HUNT	22
IV.	THE COTSWOLD HUNT	35
V.	THE NEW FOREST HUNT	46
VI.	THE TEDWORTH HUNT	79
VII.	THE HURWORTH HUNT	101
VIII.	NORTON CONYERS	125
IX.	SIR BELLINGHAM GRAHAM, BART.	149
X.	ATHERSTONE—PYTCHLEY—QUORN	168
	INDEX	201

LIST OF ILLUSTRATIONS

	PAGE
SIR REGINALD GRAHAM, BART.	*Frontispiece*
THE EIGHTH DUKE AND DUCHESS OF BEAUFORT	13
COLONEL MILES, ON BLUE PILL	15
LADY BLANCHE SOMERSET ON VIOLET	18
LORD HENRY BENTINCK	22
MR. HENRY CHAPLIN, M.P.	24
THE REV. JOSEPH PITT, VICAR OF RENDCOMB	43
COLONEL MARTIN POWELL	65
HOUND SHOW AT PETERBOROUGH	67
MR. THOMAS ASSHETON SMITH	80
LORD ALGERNON ST. MAUR	89
LADY GRAHAM	123
THE HALL AT NORTON CONYERS	127
VISCOUNT ANDOVER (AFTERWARDS EARL OF SUFFOLK) AND SIR REGINALD GRAHAM, BART.	146
SIR BELLINGHAM GRAHAM'S TREACLE	155
SIR BELLINGHAM GRAHAM, BART., ON THE BARON	159

FOX-HUNTING RECOLLECTIONS

CHAPTER I

EARLY DAYS

How I envy the facile pen which let us into the secrets of *Market Harborough*, and told us of Tilbury Nogo, that unsuccessful man so admirably described by George Whyte - Melville. What would I not give for the ever-pleasant pencil with which the Druid jotted down the plain, unvarnished words of Dick Christian, as that veteran hero personally conveyed him in a one-horse gig along the bridle roads of Leicestershire ? Classic names are these, recalling to many of us the old days, and that sensation of screaming delight with which we once galloped for a start. To-day, such musings are all in vain, for it is at a snail's pace, and in chastened mood, that I approach my formidable task.

Memoirs are often prefaced by unnecessary reference to parentage and pedigree ; this at least shall not be laid to my charge. Was not that old lady justified in her bitter reproof to a young man overfond of allusions to his family? "Don't talk to me of ancestors," she said; "I once kept a grandmother myself!" Let it be sufficient to record that 1835 was the year of my birth at Norton Conyers, in the North Riding of Yorkshire; that I was educated at the Royal Military College, Sandhurst, gazetted at the age of seventeen to the 14th Regiment (then the Buckinghamshire, now the West Yorkshire), joined them at Limerick, passed a year in Ireland, and at the end of that period was ordered with the regiment to Malta. The detachment with which I went sailed in an old troopship of about seven hundred tons, by name the *Alipore*, and it took fifteen days on the voyage from Cork to Gibraltar (think of that in these days of swift military transport).

Malta was but a brief halting-place on the way to the Crimea, and we landed at Balaclava the first week of November 1854. The 14th was soon moved to the front, and posted to the Third Division, commanded by General Sir Richard England. Our chief duty for many months to come was in the trenches day and night, and my most vivid recollection of that dreary time is snow, everlasting snow, throughout the bitterly severe winter of 1854–55. Owing to our hasty

FOX-HUNTING RECOLLECTIONS 3

departure from Malta we, like the rest of the army, were ill-provided with suitable clothing, and I remember the joy with which I received at last a fur coat and a pair of long brown boots sent out from England, ready-made and not exactly a perfect fit; but to me at that time they were beyond all price. I kept well, and was as happy as the day was long (the days were rather long in the trenches); but soon after Sebastopol was evacuated by the Russians on the 8th September 1855, I had a very bad turn of Crimean fever, and was sent down to the hospital at Scutari, where my head was shaved, and for some weeks it seemed doubtful how matters would end for me. Our chief interest in hospital was to watch for Florence Nightingale as she passed through the wards with a gentle word for all,—a weary time until I improved and was invalided to England towards the end of 1855. My Crimean experience was at the age of from nineteen to twenty, and, looking back to such distant times, it seems to me nowadays as if those scenes had been in another world, and I feel myself a veritable Rip Van Winkle as I muse upon those far-off days and wonder how many officers still survive who landed at Balaclava with the old Fighting Fourteenth on that November day in 1854.

February 1856 found me gazetted to the Rifle

Brigade as Captain at twenty years of age, and almost the youngest Captain in the British Army. I joined the depôt of the 2nd Battalion at Aldershot, and my chief remembrance of that spot is in complete contrast to that of the Crimea : eternal field days instead of the trenches, and perpetual dust instead of snow. Upon the whole I much preferred Crimean life.

Another recollection of that period is the enthusiasm about pugilism which animated a few young officers in various regiments then stationed in the camp at Aldershot. Willingly was I enlisted in that select circle, prominent among whom was a Second Lieutenant of the 60th Rifles, now a distinguished General ; also two officers of that famous regiment the 16th Lancers, who are still flourishing ; there may have been a few others whose names are now forgotten. Many prize-fights within reach did we attend, and more than once we left by a night train to assist early the following morning at what *Bell's Life* was wont to term " A Merry Mill in the Midlands." Cock-fighting was also to be seen at that time, more especially in the neighbourhood of Hendon, a battle-ground well known to some of us. These Corinthian pursuits, which were in favour full fifty years ago, have long since been extinguished —such tastes and attractions are to-day obsolete

FOX-HUNTING RECOLLECTIONS 5

as the history of Tom and Jerry—and extinct as Pierce Egan himself.

Early in 1857 I was appointed aide-de-camp to General Sir Richard England, who commanded the troops in the district of the Curragh of Kildare, and was there until 1858, when I was ordered to join the 4th Battalion of the Rifle Brigade at Chichester, a new battalion just raised and organised by Colonel Elrington, a very smart Rifleman. From Chichester Barracks some of us used to hunt with Colonel Wyndham's hounds (Squires was his huntsman), in what afterwards became the Goodwood Country. Colonel Wyndham was created Lord Leconfield in 1859, died in 1869, and was succeeded by his son Henry Wyndham of the 1st Life Guards (a lifelong friend of mine), who became the second Lord Leconfield and reigned at Petworth as M.F.H. until his lamented death in 1901. Sheppard, his huntsman, was one of the best in his profession, and a particularly nice man.

The 4th Battalion was ordered out to Malta, and landed there in August 1858. The following spring I again went on the Staff as aide-de-camp to General Sir Gaspard Le Marchant, who was then Governor and Commander-in-Chief of the Island. With him I remained until His Excellency went to England, where we arrived in May 1860. On my part there was no regret at leaving Malta—my final farewell might have been said in the words of Byron:

"Adieu ye joys of La Valette,
Adieu sirocco, sun, and sweat,
Adieu thou palace rarely entered,
Adieu ye mansions where I've ventured,
Adieu ye cursed streets of stairs,
How surely he who mounts them swears!"

In the autumn of 1860 I was posted to the Rifle Depôt at Winchester, commanded by Colonel Macdonald. No better quarter in England than old Winchester—so many sports, pastimes, and advantages; dry fly fishing in the Test and Itchen, nowadays at famine prices, was to be got for next to nothing in those days. How many delightful afternoons did I pass on the water of Brambridge House, then belonging to Charles Sartoris—how many games of tennis in the old tennis-court at Crawley, the Queen's Crawley of Thackeray in *Vanity Fair*. I never could see that tumbledown old house (since demolished altogether) without thoughts of Rawdon Crawley, Becky Sharp, and Hester's famous speech, "If you please, Sir Pitt, Sir Pitt died this morning, Sir Pitt." Then the hunting (our Colonel was very good about leave for that), and plenty of packs to choose from: the H.H., with Edward Tredcroft as Master; the Hambledon, hunted by

Walter Long of Preshaw; the Vyne, by Lord Portsmouth; and the Hursley, with Mr. Tregonwell as Master. The last was a squire from Dorsetshire; such a trim little man between fifty and sixty, always in faultless costume, with boots and breeches worthy of a better country, rather deaf and very silent. While at a hunt breakfast in the barracks some young spark (with doubtful taste) stuffed his horn with buttered toast, but even the discovery of this indignity he endured in complacent silence. A few years ago I accidentally came across his tombstone in a Bournemouth churchyard, where he has been resting for many years. When we could not leave barracks until after morning parade there was a pack of harriers which could always be found, and was never far away, hunted by old James Dear, a brewer at Winchester. Another pack was kept by John Day, the well-known trainer at Danebury, near Stockbridge, but these were more difficult to reach. Mr. Nevill of Chilland kept a few couples of black St. Hubert hounds and a tame deer or two; he was much deformed, and obliged to ride in a kind of basket chair on the top of his saddle. On hunting mornings the whole party went to the appointed fixture; the deer was given a generous start, and ran until captured by the St. Huberts. When the hunt was over, the Master, with his quaint establishment, the deer and the hounds, all trotted home together ; they seemed to be a kind of happy family who lived on friendly terms and were mutually pleased with one another, a bright example of domestic life. For all these variations of the chase, hunters of more or less value could be procured from John Tubb, the widely known dealer who resided opposite to the barrack gates, a man with much resource of language and a certain amount of notoriety peculiar to himself. He was periodically out of favour with many racecourse authorities, but as a universal provider of horseflesh, and as a very original character, he was well known to most Riflemen when stationed at the depôt. In that pleasing work, *The Queen's Hounds*, Lord Ribblesdale, well acquainted with his subject, devotes some pages to episodes in John Tubb's career.

At what pleasant country houses we used to stay : Warnford Court, where lived Mr. and Mrs. Edward Sartoris—she had been Adelaide Kemble ; and there we frequently met her elder sister, Mrs. Butler, who preferred to be still known by her former name, Fanny Kemble. They were the daughters of Charles Kemble and nieces of Mrs. Siddons, and both were gifted with dramatic talents and singular attractions. Adelaide had been very celebrated as a prima donna in London and in many foreign capitals from 1835, when she appeared as Norma at Covent Garden, until the close of her stage career in 1842. Who has not read her charming story, *A Week in a French Country House*? Fanny had been the greatest actress of her time, and had played Juliet at the age of seventeen. But is not all this related by her own pen in *Records of a Girlhood*? Here also were to be found Leighton, Val Prinsep, Henry Greville, George Barrington, Hamilton Aidé, and Miss Thackeray, long before she became Mrs. Ritchie. How well I remember the charm of that society, and those memorable evenings when Adelaide Sartoris would sing with touching expression and a voice still entrancing; Fanny Kemble would recite in deep, tragic tones; and Edward Sartoris himself would sometimes relax sufficiently to read (as no one else could read) the plays of Shakespeare which he knew so well.

Then the Grange, where at that time lived the second Lord and Lady Ashburton. I was often there, and met many celebrities—Landseer, the Carlyles, Sir Roderick Murchison, Charles Kingsley, Venables (of the *Saturday Review*), Laurence Oliphant, the Brookfields, and others. I have a pleasant memory of Kingsley in particular—in complete contrast to Carlyle as a social factor, whose return to the ordinary salutation of "good-morning" was at least abrupt, and hardly encouraging to further conversation. Mrs. Carlyle, on the contrary, never ceased to talk in a strident voice with broad Scotch accent. A comet in this circle was the Honourable James Macdonald, whom I first met at the Grange, little thinking I should have the good fortune to know him so intimately in future years. To all the world he was Jim Macdonald; to the last Duke of Cambridge he was Military Secretary and Equerry for nearly forty years, with a sunny face bubbling with merriment, hair like white satin, and a voice like a silver bell; the fascination of his company was indeed irresistible. Brookfield was very agreeable, with a knack of putting a humorous construction upon the most simple matters of fact. He was supposed to be the original of Thackeray's Charles Honeyman in the *Newcomes*, though I could never quite recognise the portrait myself. Anyhow, Thackeray must have known the Brookfields well, inasmuch as it is on record that he was a guest at the first dinner-party of their early days, when the hostess modestly asked if she might help him to a tartlet, and the great novelist, grasping the situation and the probability of an adjacent pastry-cook, quietly replied, "If you please, and pray give me a twopenny one."

CHAPTER II

THE BEAUFORT HUNT

IN the spring of 1863 I was still at Winchester Barracks, and obtained leave of absence for a month in order to join an expedition which was then being organised to hunt wolves in the South of France. The Duke of Beaufort took out twenty-two couples of doghounds and his hunting establishment to Poitou, where a good-sized house with stabling and temporary kennels had been engaged for him eight miles from Poitiers. His party comprised the Honourable Henry Wyndham, the Honourable Edward Russell, Lord Worcester (then sixteen and still at Eton), and myself. We all arrived early in April in most unfavourable weather for the purpose—a blazing sun every morning, very dry, and no prospect of rain. The country was composed of large woods surrounded by expansive plains chiefly devoted to vineyards. We were out three days a week, and at the fixtures generally by eight or nine in the morning. The animal was difficult to find, and altogether we had little success owing to the heat and other circumstances. There was also the drawback that some of the hounds did not relish the idea. An obstinate old fellow called " Foiler " positively declined to hunt the wolf at all, and was consequently left at home. Two or three couples decided to vote with " Foiler," and only one young wolf was killed during the month. One really fine run out there, however, is worthy of record. An old wolf had been seen to enter an immense wood at daybreak; the Duke on his way to hunt was told of this, and decided to draw for him with the whole pack (tufting had hitherto been tried most days), so as to force him to face the open. The plan succeeded—the wolf broke away, ran quite straight for eight or ten miles—in a cloud of dust never more than half a mile before the pack, and evidently with no idea of being caught that day. At last he ran through a plantation full of roe deer which jumped up in view, and away went the hounds after them. By the time they were got together again the wolf was gone, the sun was out, and the hunt was over.

From all parts of France sportsmen flocked to Poitou, and there were large fields in consequence. At the end of April the establishment returned to England, and our party stayed a day or two in Paris, where the Duke was entertained

THE 8TH DUKE AND DUCHESS OF BEAUFORT
1864

at a banquet and made a charming speech in excellent French. On the whole there had not been much sport as regards wolf-hunting, but it was an interesting expedition under most pleasant auspices.

During this year I retired from the Army, and for some seasons afterwards hunted with the Beaufort Hunt—an immense extent of territory, combining almost every description of country—with more than ample for six days a week. At that time three distinct packs were maintained; Clark was huntsman, and Jack West and Heber Long whipped in; they were all in green plush, which looked smart enough in fine weather, but was rather apt to hold the wet. Members of the Hunt wore the well-known Blue and Buff, for which distinction ladies also were in great competition. The country always seemed to be full of foxes, and there was no end of sport with them. Many merry spins over the walls, and many a good day's sport did I enjoy with the Blue and Buff.

The fastest gallop I ever saw in this country was on the 12th December 1864. They found him in Pacey's Plantation, rather a flying start, and only two or three got away with the hounds; they raced a tremendous pace for forty-two minutes by Crudwell, across Paradise Farm and the meadows near Eastcourt House, over the brook to the fourteen acres at Braydon; there, I think, we got among fresh foxes. It was a lucky day for me, as I had a front seat all the way.

Colonel Poulett Somerset had mounted me on a well-bred chestnut horse called Happy Land, which he purchased from Ben Land, the steeplechase trainer. I bought the horse the next day and renamed him Paradise, but he soon became "Paradise Lost," as he was one of five hunters which Granville Somerset bought in a lump from me for £500 one evening towards the end of that season.

Clark resigned suddenly in 1868, and from that time Lord Worcester (then just come of age) hunted the hounds. The celebrated Great Wood run, in which he so much distinguished himself, took place on 21st February 1871. The late Duke's fame was known to all the world as the best of sportsmen and the kindest of friends; by nature he was endowed with courtesy and other attributes which rendered him a most popular Master of Hounds, and no one who hunted with him for a single day could fail to notice his never-failing exertions to show sport. Weather made no difference to him, and his hounds seldom went home until dusk; his dog language and hunting

COLONEL MILES, ON "BLUE PILL"
1870

FOX-HUNTING RECOLLECTIONS 15

voice were quite unequalled, and he was the best horn-blower I ever listened to. At all times most particular about tail hounds being cut off in chase, it was woe betide the young gentleman whom he saw slip through a gate without first giving the chance to a hound or two who might perhaps have had a bad start. Prominent among the forward riders of the sixties were Colonel Kingscote (now Sir Nigel), Colonel Miles, and Bob Chapman, the noted horsedealer from Cheltenham, whom no one could beat over the walls. Colonel Miles had been in the 17th Lancers, and was generally known as Peter Miles. Always a welter-weight, he had as a young man made a reputation in Leicestershire, where he attracted the admiration of Sir Richard Sutton, Master of the Quorn from 1846 to 1855. Mr. Bromley Davenport, M.P., illustrates that charming book entitled *Sport* with various sketches of his model champion negotiating oxers and sailing over ridge and furrow. At another period he also immortalised Peter Miles in verse, rather at the expense of the author's old friend, Mr. W. L. Gilmour, once a celebrated Meltonian, but a little going off at the time of Colonel Miles's advent.

" Wait till the second horseman pass,
You'll see a form, 'tis his, alas!

The heavy man who funks the stiles,
And shudders at the name of Miles.

Such is the fate of mortal man,
Where Gilmour ended, Miles began,
And Miles in turn must yield his sway,
For every dog shall have his day."

Another fine horseman was Captain Little (the Josey Little of Chandler fame), always ready for a gallop. It was whispered about, that once upon a time he had ridden gallantly to a single hound who raced away on a line by himself for five minutes, when the Captain jumped on the hound, killed him on the spot, and his private run came to an untimely end. I presume he had long since expiated that offence, for he was frequently out with the hounds in my time.

An excellent sportsman was Granville Somerset, Q.C. (widely known as the Doctor), who hunted there every winter; a short, stout man with a pleasant countenance, who wore an unusual number of waistcoats, and was devoted to the Chase—generally a stern chase for him.

We often went together to hunt on Exmoor with the Devon and Somerset staghounds.

Dulverton, Porlock, and Minehead were our various headquarters, and we sometimes stayed with our mutual friend the Master of the Pack, Mr. Fenwick Bissett, at Bagborough, near

FOX-HUNTING RECOLLECTIONS 17

Taunton (who had formerly been an officer in the King's Dragoon Guards) a man of huge frame, with strong character and much determination and perseverance.

Enthusiastic on the subject, he undertook the task of reviving the Chase of the Wild Red Deer in North Devon and West Somerset, and was Master of the Staghounds from 1855 to 1881 with very successful results.

He died in 1883 when about sixty years of age, and was buried in the churchyard at Bagborough.

Granville Somerset was a Queen's Counsel with an immense amount of Parliamentary practice at the Bar, and how he got through all his business and made a fortune as well was a wonder to all, for he was to be seen with hounds in autumn, winter, and spring, beginning on Exmoor and ending in the New Forest; but wherever he went he was always welcome as a most genial companion.

What a delightful place to stay at was Badminton! Full of guests throughout the winter, and unlimited hospitality, surely there never existed a more kindly couple than that warm-hearted Duke and his good Duchess! How fond of hunting, too, was their only daughter Lady Blanche, so universally beloved! She married in 1874 the 5th Marquis of Waterford, and, sad indeed to relate, died after a long illness in 1895.

It is many years now since I wore a blue and buff coat, but time cannot efface recollections of the friendship and fox-hunting which were my experience with the Beaufort Hunt.

In 1865 I had two or three steeplechasers trained by Saunders at Hednesford. The best of them was Marble Hill, by Teddington, a horse I bought at Tattersall's when Lord Uxbridge's stud was sold. He proved a good investment that spring, as within a few weeks of the purchase he won the Croydon Steeplechase and Hurdle Race on consecutive days ; George Ede rode him then and subsequently, when he won several hunt races for me.

In 1867 I bought Romping Girl, by Wild Dayrell, from old John Osborne—a three-year-old which had just run second for the Oaks ; she went to Findon to be trained with Lord Westmorland's string by William Goater, a capital trainer of the old-fashioned school. That autumn the mare was in the Cesarewitch with seven stone. Sammy Kenyon rode her, and her chance was much fancied, but she only got third in a very large field. During the next two years she won a

LADY BLANCHE SOMERSET, ON "VIOLET"
1870

FOX-HUNTING RECOLLECTIONS 19

great many races, and in 1869 I was elected a member of the Jockey Club.

Stirring times they were indeed on the Turf in the sixties; it was then that Mr. Henry Chaplin first appeared with Breadalbane and Broomielaw, and subsequently won the memorable Derby of 1867 with Hermit, by Newminster; about the same time came the rapid and sensational career of the 4th and last Marquis of Hastings, ending with his early death in 1868 when only twenty-six.

Other racing magnates of those days were Prince Sotykoff, General Peel, Mr. Stirling Crauford, Lords Glasgow, Stamford, Coventry, Falmouth, Ailesbury, Chesterfield, Portsmouth, and Wilton; the Dukes of Beaufort, Hamilton, and Newcastle; Baron Rothschild, Count La Grange, Count Batthyany, Mr. Ten Brock, Colonel Towneley, Messrs. Sturt, Bowes, Sutton, Pryor, Jardine, Sir Frederick Johnstone, and Sir Joseph Hawley, who won the Derby four times and was known as " the lucky Baronet."

Much in evidence also were the three " Romeo Lords," Courtenay, Howard, and Andover, a well-known trio who lived to become Earls of Devon, Effingham, and Suffolk; but they all three died comparatively early, and with the last-named I lost one of my greatest friends.

The sixties were also essentially the racing

era of Admiral Rous and George Payne, and being constantly at Newmarket I knew them both intimately. Scores of times did I dine with the old Admiral and Mrs. Rous at their house on the Terrace. A memorable feature at those parties was the matchmaking which was sure to come off when the claret had been round two or three times. Two or more of the guests would ask the Admiral to handicap their respective horses for the purpose; and, ever ready for this kind of business, he first made a proviso that each owner should hold half a crown in his closed fist. After some minutes' reflection the handicapper in solemn tones proclaimed the course and the weights. The hands were opened; if no money, no match; but if the half-crowns were still there, then it was a match; the half-crowns passed into the Admiral's pocket, and all three were satisfied. Nobody seems to drink claret nowadays, and the only matches wanted after dinner are for the inevitable cigarette.

On the Heath in those times we all rode hacks or ponies. The winning-post was dragged from one spot to another, rather like a portable bathing machine. There were ropes along the courses, and this continued until one evening at dusk Colonel Blackwood, a Queen's Messenger, rode against the ropes; the horse fell and broke

FOX-HUNTING RECOLLECTIONS

his rider's neck. After this the authorities thought it high time to substitute white posts and rails for the old ropes, and more modern stands were erected.

Who that once knew George Payne could ever forget him? A man of Herculean frame, with emphatic voice and expression, whose company was much sought for; jovial and humorous, with a fund of strange anecdotes, frequently against himself. I never saw him anywhere except in frock-coat with high hat and the inevitable deep neckcloth of black and white (his racing colours). Twice Master of the Pytchley, and an owner of racehorses ever since he came of age in 1825, he started with a large fortune in addition to his Sulby estate in Northamptonshire, but there was little left in his later years. Still, no misfortunes could damp his spirits; to the end he remained gay and joyous as ever, and it might have been said of him when he died in 1878 that his motto for life had been

"Laugh, and the whole world will laugh with you;
Sigh—and you may sigh alone."

CHAPTER III

THE BURTON HUNT

ANOTHER country in which I often hunted formerly was the Burton, at the time when it was a six-days-a-week hunt, and long before the Blankney as a separate country was ever thought of. Lord Henry Bentinck had been Master from 1842 to 1864, and it was towards the close of his reign that I first made acquaintance with the celebrated pack which he had formed. It was composed chiefly of Grove, Belvoir, and Brocklesby blood, with several strains from Osbaldeston's famous hounds. Their chief characteristics were drive, speed, stoutness, and extreme quality; in appearance the doghounds were perhaps a little light of bone, but they were never known to tire. All this was the result of a master mind devoted for over twenty years to the study of hound-breeding. The art of handling them in the field was also brought to perfection in Lord Henry's time: noise, hallos, whip-cracking, and over-riding were his especial abominations. In the days to which I allude Charley Hawtin was the huntsman, a bright, talented

LORD HENRY BENTINCK
1862

man who carried out his Master's theories to the letter. He had a bad fall on his head and was never quite the same afterwards, but he came to me in the New Forest in 1875 and remained in my service until he died in 1877. The whippers-in were Harry Dawkins, W. Goodall (afterwards with the Pytchley), W. Smith (still with the Bramham Moor), and as a quartet of hunt servants they were probably never surpassed. Will Goodall (at Belvoir) and Dick Burton (formerly with Osbaldeston) appear to have been Lord Henry's models upon which he based his system of hunting hounds in the field. About his own achievements Lord Henry was singularly reticent, and, when asked as to the secret of his success in hound-breeding, he curtly replied: "I breed a great many hounds and I hang a great many."

After Lord Henry came Viscount Doneraile from Ireland, for a season or two, and then in 1866 Mr. Henry Chaplin at the age of twenty-five became the Master, purchasing the pack for a large sum and hunting the Burton country six days a week. Always a heavy-weight and rather short-sighted, but gifted with heaven-born hands, no one could beat the Squire of Blankney over Wellingore or any other country. With a natural knowledge of hunting, a quick eye for hounds in or out of the kennel, and marvellous memory for their pedigrees and breeding, he frequently hunted the pack himself with much success. His establishment was on a magnificent scale, and such hunters as his Emperor and Snowstorm were, perhaps, never seen. Genial, generous, and kind-hearted, he was ever anxious that his countless friends should share the sport and entertainment which he could so well provide. For several winters I passed many weeks under his hospitable roof either at Blankney, or at his perfect hunting-box, Burghersh Chauntry, in the town of Lincoln. He remained Master until 1871, when the country was divided; the Burton and Blankney then becoming two separate hunts. Mr. F. J. S. Foljambe (of Osberton) became Master of the Burton, and Colonel Edward Chaplin, formerly of the Coldstream Guards, took charge of the Blankney until 1877, when the Squire reappeared on the scene as M.F.H. until 1881, and then he sold most of his hounds to Lord Lonsdale. Some years later on, the whole pack was sold by auction at Rugby, dispersed in lots, and scattered in all directions.

Sometimes we find in the *Field* newspaper the inquiry, " Where are the descendants of Lord Henry's celebrated pack ? " A question which may well be asked, for as regards foxhound blood

MR. HENRY CHAPLIN, M.P.

FOX-HUNTING RECOLLECTIONS 25

it was almost a national calamity in the hunting world when such a famous pack was dispersed at the hammer. Lord Chesham bought largely at the Rugby sale, in addition to which he purchased from me every Blankney bitch that I possessed on retiring from the Hurworth country in 1888 (I had bought about eighteen couples privately from Lord Lonsdale a few years previously).

When Lord Chesham gave up the Bicester country there was probably more of the real blood in that kennel than in any other. No doubt the sort may still exist in other kennels, but it would be interesting to know where it most abounds. Where, indeed, are the descendants of Contest, Regulus, Damper, Dorimont, Vanquisher, Tapster, Sailor, and Saladin? Let those who have the blood value it as priceless, for now it could not be obtained for love or money.

When I was hunting the New Forest in 1874, I had about twenty couples from Mr. Chaplin, and my bitch pack was in those days, and again in the Hurworth country in 1886, composed of that blood. I never knew one of them to tire. Who that ever saw the pack when in Lord Henry's hands, and hunted by Charley Hawtin, can forget how at the end of the longest day they would cast themselves one or two fields in front of their huntsman and fling themselves at a gallop in a semicircle until they recovered the line? Lord Henry devoted a lifetime and his great talents to the breeding of hounds, but he well knew that his labour was in vain unless they were carefully and judiciously handled in the field. Every detail of information was recorded daily in his private kennel book, and on reference to its contents many passages are to be found showing the remarkably acute observation with which he watched the performance of his pack—for instance :

" Comus, 1844. A model little dog; a very hard runner.

" Tomboy, 1845. Got the name of the Schoolmaster of the pack, and was probably the best and most sagacious dog that ever ran in the Midland counties. These two dogs ran in the bitch pack. There was little to choose between them—in nose, brilliancy, or stoutness; each dog was equally quick in dropping clear into the dry ditches and working a dying fox out of them. But Comus could be led wrong by wild men or a flashing pack of hounds; while neither man, nor hound, nor fox could make a fool of Tomboy. However wild men or hounds might be, he would quickly leave them and turn back to his fox. Nothing could put him out of temper, and in his last season he could still race with puppies at night.

" Contest, 1848. A model dog, a most brilliant

FOX-HUNTING RECOLLECTIONS

animal; noted for his hard running, flying the gates and double rails without touching them, and, too, for turning short without the need of a 'drag chain.'

"Comrade, 1849. A capital dog, not so showy in his work as

"Contest, a quicker dog, shorter in his neck, and not perfectly clever about his knees. He missed, from accidents, a great deal of his work as a one and two-year-old.

"Craftsman, 1849. The best finder of a fox that ever came into the kennel; rather slack in his loins, and until three years old a very delicate dog.

"Ruler, 1850. This was an extraordinary brilliant dog, a very hard runner, and remarkable for the distance he could bring his hounds back to the spot where they last had it good; and for working the dry ditches, old Rosebud's excellence came out in him.

"Challenger, 1853. A capital and model dog in appearance—died suddenly. A terrible loss.

"Corsair, 1854. This dog nearly equalled Tomboy in sagacity; a brilliant animal in every respect.

"Titian, 1858. A most brilliant and determined dog—a terrible savage when a fox was killed; so were his two sons.

"Trinket, 1856. A capital hound, noted for her Tomboy sagacity.

"Ringworm, 1856. Noted for jumping out

of the very centre of the pack in full cry when hunting it heelway—turning back and never being caught for two miles in the Gainsboro' Woods.

"Sontag, 1860. Noted for taking the hounds through two miles of sheep, driving before them along the Clakby hillside in the great Wickenby run.

"Riot, 1861. Followed by her sister Ruby, is noted for having taken back her huntsman and hounds three large fields to the spot where they left their fox in Thornly. A very brilliant performance.

"Dainty, 1863. Noted for showing up all the old hounds as a puppy in a dry ditch; destroyed by kennel lameness.

"Regulus, 1861. A very good dog; noted for working the roads and dry ditches.

"Regent, 1861. Noted for taking his hounds through sheep. The most brilliant dog of the two; died suddenly.

"Victor and Vaulter, 1861. Two very brilliant dogs; little to choose between them. Especially noted for jumping the gate out of the Rasen Road and racing back three large fields with their heads up to the dry ditch where a dying fox had been left in the great Wickenby run. A brilliant performance."

A great number of the Grove hounds were purchased at Mr. Foljambe's sale in 1845, and the following remarks appear about them :—

"The dogs purchased at this sale made the pack.

"Driver, Stranger, Streamer, were three capital dogs, and all ran until seven and eight years old. All three were remarkable for this—that when beaten off from pace in their old age, they would come up behind as quiet as mice, set to work at once as busily as bees and help the young ones out of their difficulties.

"Driver was noted for bringing the fox's brush to his huntsman' out of Harpswell gorse. His son Desperate showed the same characteristic. A fox having been left in a rabbit-hole in Carlton sand hills, the hounds being called away, Desperate gave the men the slip, went back to the hole and scratched down to his cub, bit off half his brush and brought it on to old Dick at Scampton.

"Driver's daughter, little Dorcas, would never allow any dog, however big, to take the head from her—she invariably carried it home any distance.

"Albion, sire of Tomboy, was not himself more than a good, honest, quiet dog, not at all brilliant.

"Royal, a big plain but brilliant dog for pace at seven years old.

"Heedless, though dam of Dorcas, was quite a third-rate animal herself.

"Careless, 1845, a most trimming animal for nose and stoutness, turned rogue at four years old.

"Rakish, 1847, never showed herself remarkably until 1851, when she appeared nearly as good as Dairymaid.

"Dairymaid, 1847. The Schoolmistress of the pack—a capital hound.

"Tomboy, Corsair, and Ruler will have been our best and wisest dogs.

"Crier and Carver, 1850. Two miserably-mean animals in appearance — capital dogs. These five Stranger puppies were noted for having been the leading hounds that coursed their second fox into Spridlington Thorns in the Great Folding hunt day."

The following notes appear on hounds purchased at Mr. Drake's sale in 1851 :—

"Hector and Herald were two good dogs until they became free of tongue.

"Smuggler, the crack dog in Drake's pack, and a most brilliant animal until he turned rogue after being brought out two days' running by Stevens.

"Despot also began very well and ended by getting wide.

"These hounds probably only went wrong from Stevens' infamous feeding, and from being brought out day after day totally unfit to run.

"Goodall picked out these hounds for me as the best stuff in Drake's kennel.

"Charon, 1851. A very good dog—many

FOX-HUNTING RECOLLECTIONS

degrees less brilliant than Crafty—quite a first-rate animal.

"Dimity, 1851. The meanest, ill-shaped little thing, but one of the very best.

"Challenger, 1853. A capital and model dog; died suddenly.

"Gamester, 1853. A good dog otherwise, but over full of tongue.

"Cardinal, 1854. A very good dog; very hard runner and good nose; never showed Corsair's wonderful sagacity.

"Pillager and Pilot, 1854, were over-full of tongue, and that tongue a very deep one. The whole litter had extraordinary good noses.

"Capable, Charmer, Clamorous, Carnage, Candid, 1854. Five brilliant and faultless animals in shape. Clara very good also, but not quite straight.

"Rufus, 1855, was a dog of remarkable sagacity, with a wonderful nose; had plenty of tongue—so had all this litter.

"Flourish, 1855. Noted for her sagacity."

Notes on hounds bought at Mr. Sutton's sale, 1856:—

"Dairymaid and Playful had undoubtedly been two good bitches with capital noses, though Bertram and Flimsey had just a turn the best of them.

"These hounds proved a useful cross in the

kennel. They were fair average hounds themselves, but neither in nose nor pace could they compete with the stuff they came amongst—save Lenity, a capital hound.

"Rambler proved very good, but we had eight or nine dogs at the time far more brilliant than him in their work.

"Playful, Trinket, Ringworm, and Castor, 1856, were four extraordinary animals.

"Traveller, 1858. Until four years old a very hard runner; almost too quiet with his tongue, and considered a rival to Tomboy and Corsair for nose and sagacity in working roads and dry ditches.

"Fed by Harry Sebright on meal and cold water, and raked and galloped about. He turned noisy and was drafted.

"Castor, Challenger, and Titian, 1856. Our three severest losses.

"Solomon and Solon, 1856. Two admirable dogs until four years, when both have been seen on three occasions to give in, nearly at the same moment. Both were very delicate hounds, and were probably never brought out by Harry Sebright fit to run.

"Wanderer, 1857, was thought shy of his tongue—a very light one and bad to hear."

It was in the Burton country I made my first attempt at hunting hounds. Late in the afternoon, when all had gone home except three or four, we had a very sharp scurry for ten or fifteen minutes after a fox almost in view, when a drain came in our way, a big jump, but on a little Irish horse of mine called Cannibal, I got well over. The dyke was probably of more formidable dimensions elsewhere, as it stopped even Mr. Chaplin, as well as Mr. Chandos Leigh and Lord Henry.

The hounds ran on for another five minutes, then threw up suddenly in the middle of a fallow field, and never touched the line again. There was no one in sight, so after a time, with all the confidence of youth, I proceeded to hold the hounds down wind and then in other directions. No doubt I must have thought it encouraging to the pack to wave my right arm with energy as I took them along with that action of the hand which is much in vogue on poultry farms. All in vain. They never touched the line again. I looked round once more; what did I see? Fifty yards behind there stood Lord Henry himself, the Messrs. Chaplin, Chandos Leigh, and Charley Hawtin. Would that the earth could have swallowed me up at that moment! Slowly, step by step, the cavalcade approached! I heard a smothered "hush" and yet another pause! At last Lord Henry, in slow, measured tones, almost hissed out word by word, "Sir Reginald, when you have quite done feeding your chickens, perhaps you will allow *my* huntsman to cast *my* hounds." I did not hear the last of it for many a day. Even now, forty years after date, I doubt if that episode is quite forgotten when I meet my good old friends the Right Honourable Henry Chaplin and Sir E. Chandos Leigh. This was my first and last effort at hunting the Burton hounds—distinctly it was not a success! The story of this adventure was fully appreciated by another intimate friend, George Whyte-Melville, who delighted in any humours of the chase, though he invariably accepted his own disasters with perfect equanimity. When living in the Pytchley country he was one day accidentally cannoned against, at a fence, by a near neighbour who had lost control of his steed, and was knocked over, horse and all. On picking himself up, and in reply to inquiries, Whyte-Melville merely remarked, "Now I know what St. Paul meant when he wrote, 'Perils by mine own countrymen.'"

CHAPTER IV

THE COTSWOLD HUNT

IN the summer of 1871 I undertook the Mastership of the Cotswold Hunt. I had long wished to become a Master of Hounds, and the opportunity occurred in consequence of the death of Mr. Cregoe Colmore, who had been Master of the Cotswold since the country was formed as a separate hunt in 1858. At the suggestion of the second Lord Fitzhardinge (well known by his nickname of "the Giant"), who had hereditary influence in that country, the Mastership of the Hunt was offered to me. I went with him to attend a General Meeting of the Cotswold Hunt, held at the Plough Hotel, Cheltenham, in June of that year, where I was unanimously elected the Master. I was promised a subscription of about £2400 a year, with an agreement on my part to hunt the country three days a week; the chief subscriber was Sir Francis Goldsmid, who lived at Rendcomb Park, and gave £500 a year; the tradesmen of Cheltenham gave a similar amount, and the remainder was contributed by the residents and visitors in the country. There was some difficulty about the hounds, as they belonged to Mr. Colmore's executors, who insisted on their being sold by auction, and the hunt horses were also sold at the same time. The sale took place at Cheltenham in July of 1871, and on behalf of the hunt committee (who raised funds for the purpose) I bought most of the pack for about nine hundred guineas. I also purchased half a dozen of the hunt horses on my own account; the remainder of my stud I got chiefly from Mr. George Reeves of Reading, a well-known horsedealer in those days. Tom Hills had been the huntsman for some time, and I re-engaged him; the new whippers-in were Dick Russell and Will Jones. Joe Titcomb became my second horseman, and I believe the latter is with them still in the same position. With forty-eight couples of hounds and about twenty horses I commenced cub-hunting on the 4th of September 1871; my headquarters were at the Plough Hotel at Cheltenham, and I had to be at the kennels (about a mile from there) every morning long before daylight in order to start with the hounds, as I did not know a yard of the country. Early in the season Tom Hills met with an accident and injured his leg, which left us in rather a fix, so I had to hunt the hounds myself, and I did so throughout most of that season.

FOX-HUNTING RECOLLECTIONS 37

On the 9th of February 1872 the Duke of Beaufort kindly invited me to bring the hounds for a day in his wall country meeting at Trouble House. We had a capital day's sport, and my diary of that time says: " Trouble House by invitation; 16½ couples. The hounds went by road to the V. W. H. kennels at Cirencester the previous night. A large field, at least five hundred horses, and many more on foot and wheels. Drew Georges Gorse blank, found at Newnton Gorse; away very fast, 35 minutes by Shipton Wood, and killed at Garden Plantation near Weston Birt. Drew the laurels at Highgrove blank, then an outlying fox jumped up; we raced him to Old Down and killed. Then halloed to a fox at Chavenage; a good hour and thirty minutes with him, but when he was quite beat a fresh fox jumped up out of a chalk pit and took us to Cherrington, where I stopped them and the hounds went home. I went with them as far as Cirencester, where I was staying with Sir William Throckmorton, who was then Master of the Vale of White Horse. There was a good scent all day, and quite a good day's sport."

At that time Bob Chapman, the noted Cheltenham horsedealer, lived at his house, Oaklands, a few minutes' walk from the kennels, and his stables were always full of high-class hunters for sale.

Many of my friends used to come and stay with me for a night or two to try their intended purchases with the Cotswold when cub-hunting. He was a capital salesman as well as a fine horseman, with the best of hands ; the nags sometimes did not go quite so smoothly when handled by the young and gilded purchasers. A great talker was Bob Chapman, and capital company at all times, especially over his own mahogany at Oaklands.

Another neighbour was Lord Coventry, who was Master of the North Cotswold, which he hunted himself with remarkable success. He had a capital lot of hounds, and was very keen to show sport and catch his foxes ; he then lived at Spring Hill near Broadway, and many a day did I enjoy with him and his hounds when he was mounted on Solferino, and his Roman, Rambler, Demon, Tradesman, and the rest of them were flying over the walls. No better judge of horse and hound then and now, no better all-round sportsman perhaps in England.

That year, 1871–72, we had a very good season ; eighty-eight days' hunting killed 21½ brace of foxes, and were stopped eight days by frost. At the end of the season Tom Hills left, and I engaged Charles Travess from the Worcestershire to come to me as K.H. and first whip, and I began my second season, 1872-73, with him, and with Will Shepherd as second whip (I think he is now huntsman in Worcestershire). We began well, and had a good time cub-hunting; but, on the 29th of November I got a bad fall. I was riding a bay mare called Gift (which I bought from Lord Coventry) in a sharp gallop over the hills: she caught the top of a wall, and gave me a smashing fall. I expect she was a bit blown at the time; anyhow, I broke the point of my right shoulder, and was laid up for many weeks in London, attended by Mr. A. Cooper (now Sir Alfred). I got back to the hounds again after a time, but was a good deal knocked about, and never quite sound for the rest of the season.

I also had an invitation day in the V. W. H. country on the 1st of April. Met at Eastcourt; a very large field there, and a scorching hot day. Found three foxes in Braydon Pond, but could do nothing with them. Lunch at Eastcourt House, and waited about till it got a bit cooler. In the afternoon we found in Oaksey Wood, and had a capital forty minutes to Cuckerdown and Kemble Wood and back to Oaksey. There for a time the hunt came to an end, and the fox seemed unaccountably lost. Being rather late everybody went home except Sir William Throckmorton and myself. I hung about for half an hour waiting for a missing hound, when my second whip trotted up to me with the hound, and whispered in my ear, " I have just seen our hunted fox." I said, " Take me to where you saw him without another word." A few yards off, in a thick hedgerow, two or three feet from the ground, sure enough there lay our fox. Out he jumped, ran into Oaksey Wood, and after a few minutes the hounds caught him. I was never so pleased in my life as I was to kill that fox, though we should not have caught him but for the intelligence of Will Shepherd. This made a good finish to a very fair day.

Three days afterwards, on the 4th of April, I had another invitation day in the Duke's country, but not with the same success as the previous year, and our sport was very moderate.

During this season we hunted eighty-nine days; killed 19 brace, and were stopped six days by frost. The fall I got in January had left its effects upon me, and I decided to resign the hounds at the end of the season, namely, on 1st of May 1873. After I left, Charles Travess was appointed huntsman, and although thirty-four years have since elapsed, he is still there in

FOX-HUNTING RECOLLECTIONS 41

that capacity, and continues to enjoy universal popularity as a huntsman of the highest class.

A few words about the history of the country. The old Earl Fitzhardinge (for many years known as Colonel Berkeley) hunted not only the present Berkeley country, but every alternate month during the season moved his hounds to the Cheltenham kennels in order to hunt both the Cotswold and the North Cotswold districts. He died in 1857, and soon after his death, his brother, Admiral Berkeley, who was created Baron Fitzhardinge in 1861, limited his country to the Cheltenham and Tewkesbury road, leaving the hills beyond Cheltenham for Mr. Colmore, who formed his pack in 1858 by buying hounds from Lord Gifford, at that time retiring from the Vale of White Horse. This arrangement continued until Lord Coventry took over the Broadway district in 1868 to create the North Cotswold, and on Mr. Colmore's death in 1871, as I have said, I succeeded him as Master of the Cotswold Hunt for two years. The pack which I hunted descended direct from Mr. Colmore's purchase.

In that wild country, where foxes are mostly stout, hounds must have speed and stamina to race up and down the hills ; also they must have drive to push a fox through the immense woodlands. The Cotswold Hills are very steep and severe, therefore hounds and horses to live with them must possess a good pedigree. The chief fences are stone walls, and formidable enough, but with a good scent hounds can race over the walls faster than most horses, jumping them abreast without that stringing and toiling after the leaders so prevalent in many countries. It must not be supposed that hounds can race every day over these wild hillsides, often enough scent is so bad that rapid progress becomes impossible ; but with a real scent and a straight fox it requires a quick man on a fast horse to keep well with hounds, for once you are away from big woods the country is, generally speaking, open and unpopulated. A very wet autumn is required to make sure of scent and sport up to Christmas ; on the other hand, there is often a screaming scent under exactly opposite conditions, and when the dust is flying in clouds in the month of March. Stout hill foxes were plentiful enough in the big woods of Withington and Chedworth in the centre of the country, as well as in the rough Cranham woodlands towards the south side, and a wild Cotswold fox once bustled in the woods will often go right away over the hills, and is not an easy animal to catch. However, the Cotswold country is not entirely hill, the exception being a strip of vale in the

THE REVD. JOSEPH PITT
Rector of Rendcomb
1872

direction of Cleeve and Uckington, where the coverts are small, and a fox found in them invariably sets his head straight for the hills, which frequently means a sharp gallop over the grass.

The features of the country most vivid in my memory are the stout breed of long grey foxes, and the splendid race of stalwart yeomen who lived upon the Cotswold Hills.

I must not forget a quaint character who had a peculiar fascination for me and many others; this was the Rev. Joseph Pitt of Rendcomb Rectory, a fox-hunting parson of the old school. At the time I speak of he was about sixty years of age, with a grim, rugged face, shaggy eyebrows, and a twinkle in his eye which betokened the fund of comic humour concealed under that weather-beaten visage. Very clerical was his costume: always a tall hat somewhat ruffled, a profusion of white neckcloth, a long black greatcoat, and inevitable umbrella, which he carried in his hand, even when mounted for the chase. In deep sonorous tones he addressed everybody as "Sir," but most of his friends called him "Joe." He was very fond of expeditions to see other hunts, especially the Duke of Beaufort's, though the difficulty for him on these occasions was to elude the vigilance of his spouse, a rather demure lady with decided views on domestic discipline, who kept an ever-watchful eye on such proceedings, and discouraged his wanderings after what she termed " strange packs of hounds." He sometimes asked me to organise a plan with him for an excursion to meet the Duke's hounds at Trouble House or Newnton Lodge, but Mrs. Pitt would be sure to get wind of it somehow, and put her foot down in opposition to the scheme.

The Reverend Joe would say, " But, my dear, I promised to pay my respects to His Grace tomorrow." To which she would reply, " Nonsense, stay at home and look after your parish." Again he pleaded, " But, my dear, you would not have me break my word " ; and sure enough the next morning would find this eminent divine at Trouble House with what I believe are called ante-gropelows over his trousers, mounted on his old bay horse (who made a noise and rejoiced in the name of Musical), pounding away all day long, popping over the walls as they came, murmuring when in the air, " Capital, sir," and on landing, " Wonderful, sir." To the last moment he would stay with them, little heeding the Trouble House he would surely find that evening on return to the Rectory.

How often have I parted with him at nightfall, jogging home with the hounds, saying, " Good-night, Joe," to which he would reply in a stage whisper, " Good-night, Sir; if you should think of a bye-day towards the end of the week, perhaps you would drop me a line, Sir, as the fish said to the angler."

Another time, somewhere towards Shrove Tuesday, " Good-night, Joe. Do you ever hunt in Lent ? " He replied, " Never, Sir, except on a Lent horse."

Then again at the end of the season, when the last day came round, " Good-bye, Joe. Wonder when we shall meet again ? " With an air of profound mystery he would answer, " Perhaps, Sir, I might have to be in the neighbourhood of Epsom, Sir, on some important business about the last week in May." I doubt if that idea ever quite came off; at least, I never saw him at the Derby, and I suspect Mrs. Pitt drew the line at a racecourse.

Later on in the evening of life this worthy couple left Rendcomb and retired to Torquay, where the quaint old Rector ended his days far away from those Cotswold Hills he loved so well.

CHAPTER V

THE NEW FOREST HUNT

THE New Forest is perhaps as good an example as could be wished of old English scenery, and after about eight hundred years it still remains the New Forest. Its boundaries may be smaller, but the main features are the same as in the days of William Rufus, and the names of the old woods, streams and plains still remain; moreover, it is almost the last of the old forests which England could boast of in former times.

What strikes most people when they first come to the New Forest is, that amidst all the changes which are going forward in these modern days, here, at least, is one place which is but little altered, and this perhaps is its greatest charm.

In former times there were many red deer in the Forest, and an old tradition has been handed down that the Royal Buckhounds came down to hunt them so far back as the month of August 1763. It seems certain that in the forties and fifties of the last century the Queen's Buckhounds came for several years in

FOX-HUNTING RECOLLECTIONS 47

the month of April for that purpose. After the Deer Removal Act of 1851 the red deer were ordered to be destroyed, and Captain Buckworth Powell of Foxlease, with Mr. Hay Morant of Brockenhurst Park, were some of the first to start a few couples to hunt them; then Mr. Grantley Berkeley, with two or three bloodhounds, killed a few, and they all gradually disappeared.

In the following years some packs of harriers came down during April to hunt the fallow deer, but the harriers were not a success. After this, Mr. Lovell of Hincheslea got occasional leave to hunt them; he took up the matter in earnest, and kept a few couples all the year round as the nucleus of a larger pack which he got together every spring for about six weeks' hunting in the Forest, and permission had to be obtained from the Crown annually for that period. Since those days the Forest has never been without a permanent pack of deerhounds, which hunt regularly throughout many months of the year. I remember one April in 1861, when I came down from Winchester Barracks, the fallow deer were hunted by Mr. Augustus Gore (formerly of the 7th Hussars), and old Captain Shedden, a former M.F.H., acted as huntsman for him, but that arrangement did not last long.

Mr. Lovell was a remarkable man, of tall, slight figure ; early in life he had been in the 1st Life Guards, during which time he lost his right arm by an accident when shooting pigeons at the Red House. Always a graceful horseman, no one could ride better through the Forest, and no one more thoroughly understood the art of hunting wild deer.

The following Proclamation is probably the first Notice of Foxhounds in the New Forest, and seems to have been published about 1770 :—

ADVERTISEMENT

" No Hounds are to be permitted to hunt in the Forest, except the Lord Warden's and the Duke of Richmond's (if he should choose to come), but in the month of April, viz. from the 1st to the 30th, both Days inclusive.

" That no Pack be suffered to go out more than three Times in one Week, and no Hounds to be taken out the intermediate Days ; and, to prevent confusion, it is agreed that the Lord Warden's Hounds are to hunt Monday, Wednesday, and Friday, and Mr. Grove's to hunt Tuesday, Thursday, and Saturday, and no more than two Packs of Hounds to be in the Forest at the same Time.

" It is necessary to remark that the Duke of Richmond had liberty from the preceding Lord Warden to bring his Hounds, which was continued

FOX-HUNTING RECOLLECTIONS

to him by the Duke of Gloucester, and was the only person who had permission to use, not only the Kennels and Stables, but the King's House likewise, if his Grace should choose to come, which is very improbable—then, any strange Pack must give way for the Time, that there may be no more than two Packs at the one Time.

"The Earths, not to be stopt till half-past four in the Morning, and no Hounds to be thrown off till five.

"The Earths, during the month of April, not to be stopt but by the Keepers or their Servants.

"The Keepers have orders not to suffer any Fires to be lighted on the Earths, or any Person to stand on the Earth to keep out the Foxes.

"No Tarriers to be taken out, or Foxes dug, in the month of April.

"Date 1789."

No doubt the first actual Master of the New Forest Foxhounds was Mr. Gilbert of Lambs Corner, now called Bartley Lodge, who became the M.F.H. from 1781 until he died in 1798. The Hunt Club appears to have been founded in 1783, when its meetings were held at Romsey, but soon afterwards were moved to Lyndhurst.

Mr. Gilbert's kennels were at Northwood, and a man named Woods was his first huntsman. He came into his service in January 1781, and, according to an old diary, in July of that year he was discharged for neglecting the hounds, but came back in October, having "made proper submission and asked pardon." In March 1790 a note is made that "the fox was lost by Wood's obstinacy," and in May of the same year he was discharged.

Notwithstanding his dismissal Woods does not seem to have done badly, as he was a man of saving habits, and when he died at Lyndhurst in 1820 his relations found after his death over a thousand pounds in his cottage, of which £39 was in silver. After Mr. Gilbert came Mr. John Compton of Minstead Manor, who had for his huntsman Thomas Sebright, the father of the famous Tom Sebright so long in the Milton Country.

In 1808 came the celebrated Mr. John Warde, who had then been an M.F.H. for thirty-five years. He had his kennels first at the King's House and afterwards at Foxlease, near Lyndhurst. Mr. Nicoll succeeded him in 1814, and was his own huntsman, keeping his hounds at the kennels where he lived in Lyndhurst, opposite to Bolton's Bench. Mr. Nicoll retired in 1828, selling his pack to Lord Kintore for £1000. After him Mr. William Wyndham took over the country, keeping his hounds at Burnford House, Bramshaw, and hunting them himself. He went on for ten

FOX-HUNTING RECOLLECTIONS 51

years, and was followed by Mr. Codrington, who also lived at Burnford House until his death in 1842. Then came Captain Shedden, formerly in the 17th Lancers, from 1842 to 1853; Mr. Theobald; Rev. E. Timson of Tatchbury Mount; Captain Morant from 1860 to 1869; and Mr. Standish for five seasons, until I took the Forest Country in the spring of 1874.

It came about in this way. I had heard that Lord Wolverton intended to bring his pack of bloodhounds from Dorsetshire to hunt the deer in the Forest; the idea of this took me down into those parts to see the fun. His pack consisted of about fifteen couple big black-and-tan hounds on a very large scale with a beautiful " cry," and they had the reputation of going a great pace over the Dorsetshire Downs when hunting carted deer. These hounds were kept at Lord Wolverton's place, Iwerne Minster, near Blandford. Whyte-Melville delighted in hunting with them, and used to speak in raptures of their performances, but from my recollection of them in the New Forest they seemed to me to be rather a failure there. They did not like the thick undergrowth in the New Enclosures, nor did they enjoy the tracts of heather land; also, they seemed to be very independent, and if there was any noise or the whip used they were apt to turn sulky for the rest of the day. I remember the first time they were out, Lord Wolverton cried out to a young sportsman who popped his whip, " For heaven's sake don't crack your whip or every one of them will go straight home." When down there during that month I heard by chance that Mr. Standish was giving up the Mastership of the New Forest Foxhounds (which he had hunted for five years), and had already agreed to sell his pack to go to Ireland. In those days, ever ready to take a fresh country, I jumped at the offer, and suddenly found myself the M.F.H. of the New Forest. At that moment the first thing I had to do was to look about for a pack of hounds; horses are easy enough to get, but to find hounds that are worth anything in a hurry is always a difficult matter. Eventually I heard that the Craven pack were for sale, and I went up to look at them near Hungerford. There were about seventy couple of all sorts and kinds, but owing to some disagreement in the Hunt they had to be sold immediately. I gave £500 for the whole lot, and sent them down to the Lyndhurst kennels. During that summer Mr. Henry Chaplin, who in those days had no end of hounds at Blankney, kindly gave me some eighteen couples, being his old and young drafts, so I found myself with at least eighty couples of hounds, very many more than I wanted. However, in the course of the summer I reduced them to about fifty couples; then I engaged Jack Goddard (a son of the old Jack Goddard) as my Kennel Huntsman and first whip, and a young fellow called Jim Reynolds from the North Hereford as second whip. I had decided to hunt the hounds myself; my whips turned out all right, and we got on well together.

That autumn of 1874 we began cub-hunting on the 11th August, but many of the mornings were terribly hot, and as an alternative I began to try afternoon cub-hunting, meeting at about 2.30 or 3, and generally going on as long as the daylight lasted. The experiment answered very well; it was seldom so hot at three or four in the afternoon as it was at seven or eight in the morning, besides which it got cooler every hour, and altogether the plan was a success in the Forest; perhaps it might not answer quite so well in other countries. Throughout the season of 1874 and 1875 we hunted ninety-six days, killed thirty-eight foxes, and were stopped twelve days by frost; the total of foxes does not sound very good, but it must be remembered that the New Forest is by far the most difficult of all countries for catching foxes. In the first place it is almost impossible to stop it properly; there are always holes and corners which nobody ever knew of before; then again, there are those innumerable drains in the New Enclosures frequently six to eight feet deep. If a tired fox drops down into one of them, and runs along it until he is out of sight and sheltered by masses of gorse and undergrowth, there he is as safe as if he was underground. Then again, in my time foxes were so plentiful there was the ever-constant chance of changing on to fresh foxes. We had excellent sport throughout my first season, and I extract from an old diary accounts of some days which may be mentioned:

"On the 10th November 1874 met at Stony Cross. Found in King's Garn and ran to Ravensnest; back by Canterton and Shave Green to Manor House; then over by Acres Down to Pound Hill, and on to Ferney Knap and Markway Bridge, where the fox got in somewhere. About an hour and a half, and a capital pace all the way; very few of the field saw the end of it.

"19th November.—Met at the Vine at Ower; drew Embley and Paultons blank; found at last in the afternoon in Shelley Bog, and hunted a ringing fox for about three hours round Embley and Paultons, and at last killed him in Romsey Common. A hard day for hounds, and it was moonlight before we got home.

"On the 16th January 1875 we met at Hilltop Gate, and after drawing a lot of woodlands blank in the morning we at last found a capital good fox at Abbotstanding, and ran a great pace across the open forest to Langley Manor and then on to Southampton Water: up to this about fifty minutes. The fox lay down on the mud, and the hounds could not reach him without sinking step by step as they got nearer to him. There were sixteen couples of doghounds out, and it was getting dusk. I was engaged to dine that night at Minstead Manor House with Mr. Henry Compton, so I left and told Jack to get hold of the fox if he possibly could. That evening, rather late, as the party were coming out of the dining-room, a footman came up to me and said, 'They have sent up from the kennels to say they got the fox after all, and Manager brought home the head.' The genial squire said to me, 'If we had only got that message five minutes sooner we would have opened another bottle of claret.'

"On the 30th March met at Stony Cross. Found at Lucas' Castle, and ran him over to Ocknell and back to the enclosure at Pugpits, where we lost him. Found at King's Garn, and ran him by Lynwood, Bramshaw, Ocknell, Broomy, to Islands Thorns, where the fox was just before us and quite done. As we went into the last enclosure a lot of young horses which were turned out in the Forest galloped into the middle of the pack. This gave the fox a chance, and we lost him after one hour and twenty minutes, most of it at a tremendous pace, without any check all the way."

We were by now well into spring, that time of year when all is smiling in the Forest. A bright gaudy morning is not generally supposed to be favourable for the chase, but in the New Forest a spring day may be quite brilliant, and at the same time as good, if not better, for hunting than in wet weather; moreover, when the country is dry, the bogs which extend for miles in some parts, begin to dry up, and on a warm day it is there a fox loves to lay and sun himself. For those who care to notice hounds drawing, it is always an interesting sight to watch them on these occasions. They sniff the air as they dash in, and they soon know well enough if he is there or not, though the secret may be kept until the old fellow jumps off the dry tussock where he has crouched until the very latest moment; then, and not till then, comes that crash and chorus which scatters all your cares to the winds.

In the April of that year, 1875, I invited the Duke of Beaufort to bring some of his hounds for a week of spring hunting, and about the middle of the month he sent down about twenty couples of doghounds to my kennels at

FOX-HUNTING RECOLLECTIONS

Furzey Lawn. Charles Hamblin was in charge of them, and Lord Worcester hunted them.

Lyndhurst, the capital of the Forest, never was so gay as then. The attraction of this novel idea brought no end of visitors. The Duke stayed with his sister, Lady Rose Lovell, at Hincheslea; Lord Worcester and Lord Arthur Somerset were with Lord and Lady Londesborough at Northerwood; Lord Vivian and Lord Strathnairn stayed with General Parker at Castle Malwood.

The duke's first meet was at Fritham on Thursday the 15th, when there were about five hundred people out on horseback and probably an equal number in carriages. They found their first fox in King's Garn enclosure, but he was headed over and over again on the Stony Cross Road. At last they got him away, and ran for about half an hour over the open through Ocknell Wood to Slufter enclosure, near Bratley Water, where they killed. In the afternoon they found again, and had a hunting run over the open Forest of over an hour, and lost him towards Somerley rather late in the day. I remember the hounds worked well, and it was quite a good day's sport.

The Duke's second day was on Monday, 19th April, at Brockenhurst Bridge. If the previous Thursday's meet drew together a concourse of sportsmen and spectators, it was certainly exceeded on the present occasion, and I find the following account of the sport, which appeared in the local papers at the time :

"The Duke of Beaufort's hounds, which have been brought into the New Forest for a few days hunting, followed up the large meet at Fritham of Thursday with a really grand gathering at Bulmer Lawn, near Brockenhurst Bridge, on Monday. The news of the presence of this famous Pack, which numbered $17\frac{1}{2}$ couples, in the New Forest country had become quickly noised abroad, and the little village of Brockenhurst was on Monday the centre of a gathering of the élite of sportsmen from this and adjacent counties. Every train arriving either from the east or west brought with it a long string of horse-boxes ; the Isle of Wight also contributing its quota *via* Lymington, and accompanying these was a concourse of lords, ladies, and gentlemen such as is rarely witnessed, especially in a country village. The Isle of Wight, the H. H., the Hambledon, the South and West Wilts, the East Dorset, and Earl Radnor's countries were respectively represented. For quite an hour before the time announced for the meet the roads in every direction converging on the Lawn were lined with vehicles, and horses, and persons on foot, until when noon had arrived there were not less than two thousand people present, the horsemen and horsewomen alone numbering some six or seven hundred. Lord and Lady Londesborough and party came from Northerwood House in a drag and four-in-hand, and the drags of Mr. E. G. Dalgety (Lockerley-hall), Mr. Rowland Cooper, Lymington, and others were also present. The Duke of Beaufort arrived soon after twelve, accompanied by Mr. Lovell, with whom and Lady Rose Lovell he had been staying at Hincheslea. Among those on horseback or in carriages we noticed the Marquis of Worcester (who hunts the pack), Lord Arthur Somerset (his brother), General Lord Strathnairn, Lord Algernon St. Maur, Lord Vivian, Lord Eslington, Sir Reginald Graham (Master of the New Forest Hunt), Sir Henry Paulet, General Parker, the Hon. H. D. Curzon, Mr. W. J. Long (Master of the Hambledon Hounds), Mr. H. Deacon (Master of the H. H.), Mr. John Harvey (Master of the Isle of Wight Hounds), Mr. H. T. Jenkinson, Mr. N. B. Smith, Mr. R. C. Bassett, Colonel Reynardson, Miss and Master Reynardson, Mr. Lambton, Mr. Gervis, Capt. Waterhouse, Captain Powell Montgomery, Mr. Merthyr Guest, Dr. Hearne, Mr. Wilder, Mr. Smith (Christchurch), Capt. Martin Powell, Mr. Henry Compton, Mr. Charles Day, Mr. C. Shrubb, Mr. W. C. D. Esdaile, Mr. E. Holloway, Mr. Duplessis, Mrs. de la Tour, Miss Carr, Mrs. Stewart, Mr. W. Farr, Mr. L. Cumberbatch, Mr. Hay Morant, Mr. Cecil Dixon, Mr. H. Day, Mr. C. Bovill Smith, Mr. Hasler, Mr. W. Greenwood, Mr. F. Bailey, Mr. W. B. Mudge, and many others.

The field was the most numerous and fashionable ever remembered, even by those who carry their recollections back to the " deer days," when the Forest was the " happy hunting-ground," and the perfect paradise of all true sportsmen. The pack started at half-past twelve, and the departure from the meet presented a sight rarely seen, and which will never be forgotten by those who witnessed it. The weather was of the finest, though somewhat too hot for hunting ; still, it tended to render the day thoroughly enjoyable to all present. The hounds were taken to the enclosure adjoining New Copse, from whence a fox was quickly halloed across the railway into Park Hill Enclosure. He ran first as if for Stubby, but, being headed by foot people, turned to the left, and came on to Bulmer Lawn at the Brockenhurst end of it ; then bearing to the right, went as if for New Park, but turned before reaching the road, and, running parallel with it, went into Park Hill Enclosure again at the Lyndhurst end. He came quickly out and went into Park grounds, where he dodged about for some time, and although viewed once or twice dead-beat, he managed to get to ground, or into a drain in the cover adjoining Pond Head, and was lost. A second fox was not found until five in the afternoon in Ipley Gorse, when he ran down Ipley Water, nearly to Hatchet Gate, turned to the right, and going through the adjoining covers ran up Culverly Water, and passed Culverly Farm, crossed the Beaulieu Road, and running through the thickly-timbered Forest adjoining, went into Frame Heath. Turning to the left he ran the length of it, and out near Lady Cross; went into the New Enclosure beyond, and through it nearly to the edge of Beaulieu Heath, and running short back retraced his steps nearly to Frame Heath, leaving which to the left he kept the thickly-timbered ground nearly as far as Pennerley Gate, where he went to ground, and thus saved his brush. The time occupied in this run was about fifty-five minutes, and although the pace was at no time good, the scent being flashy and wanting altogether in the Enclosures, yet it gave the hounds an opportunity of showing their hunting qualities, which they did to perfection. Excellent sport has also been obtained during the last and the previous week with both the New Forest Deerhounds and the New Forest Foxhounds. The latter pack, hunted by Sir Reginald Graham, had an extraordinary fast run of about an hour to ground at Knightwood on Saturday the 17th April."

In those days there were about half a dozen Crown keepers, who each had a large district under his charge. I found them all capital in the way of preserving foxes, and obliging about the earth stopping, which was always a very difficult matter to perform. The oldest keeper at that time was George Cooper, who lived at Bolderwood and had been in that service under the Crown for nearly fifty years; he was always out with the hounds on the north side of the Forest, and an excellent man in every way.

That famous M.F.H., Mr. Osbaldeston, after a turn with the Quorn and the Burton, took over the Pytchley Country in 1827, and during that season he is said to have exclaimed, "I have been looking for Paradise all my life and I have found it at last." I could not say quite so much as that, but I certainly was delighted with my first season in the Forest, as sport had been so good, my hounds had turned out very well, and the little pack had long since earned the name of the "Fast Ladies." They were composed of what I got from Blankney and from the Craven. Some of the latter were not quite so reliable as the former, but they were all hard runners and went a tremendous pace. Then Mr. Laurence Cumberbatch, the Deputy Surveyor who had control under the Crown of the whole Forest territory, was a good supporter to me. He was fond of all sport, but I knew he was a keen fox-hunter at heart, and was a gentleman for whom I had the greatest regard.

The area of the Forest proper in those days was about 66,000 acres, surrounded on all sides by large estates belonging to various country gentlemen. On the south side there was Beaulieu, an

FOX-HUNTING RECOLLECTIONS 63

estate of about 8800 acres, belonging to Lord Henry Scott (who afterwards was created Lord Montagu); there was also Cadland, with a large extent of woods, then belonging to Mr. Edgar Drummond; farther on there was the Exbury estate, where at that time resided Sir George Stucley, who hunted regularly with me; also Hinton Admiral, a considerable property belonging to Sir George Meyrick (whose eldest son eventually succeeded me as the Master). On the west was Bistern and its big woodlands, belonging to Mr. John Mills, who started a pack of harriers while I was there. On the north side was Hale Park, belonging to Mr. Goff; and on the east there was Paultons, belonging to old Mr. Sloane Stanley; then Embley Park; and farther away still came Broadlands, at that time owned by Mr. Cowper Temple, whom I have seen out with the hounds, but he was generally engaged in rather more serious matters of Church and State. There was also a large woodland tract on the outskirts of the Forest in the Salisbury direction, called the Earldoms, which in those days was jointly hunted by Lord Radnor and myself; but foxes were by no means plentiful in those parts, and I did not meet there more frequently than I could help. In the centre of the Forest was the well-known Minstead Manor, where lived that model country gentleman

Mr. Henry Compton, an excellent fox-preserver and the most kind and hospitable of men. I constantly stayed there as his guest, and no words can say how good he was to me; the first year or two of my time he used to come out with the hounds, especially on the north side, which was the part both he and I liked best; and as long as he kept on hunting he remained fairly well. The Chairman of the Hunt was Sir Henry Paulet, who lived at Testwood, an excellent Chairman, with tact and sound judgment. Old General Parker, who had formerly commanded the 1st Life Guards and lived at Castle Malwood, was constantly out, though as a rule the pace he went was hardly equal to the occasion, and he was often heard to say, "Sir Reginald's 'Fast Ladies' are a bit too fast for me." Other members of the Hunt in my time were Captain Buckworth Powell, who owned Foxlease, just outside Lyndhurst; he had formerly been in the Grenadier Guards and always owned a racehorse or two. Lord Normanton often came out from Somerley, his place near Ringwood. Mr. Bradburne of Lyburn, a good sportsman and a great friend of mine, who many years later took over the hounds. Captain Timson of Tatchbury, who had been in the Carabiniers. Captain Morant also sometimes appeared for

Colonel Martin Powell
1899

FOX-HUNTING RECOLLECTIONS 65

a day or two; he had been M.F.H. when I first used to come down from Winchester Barracks in the sixties, a silent man who rode the Forest very well, and I always looked upon him as quite the best Forest huntsman I ever saw.

Mr. William Everett of Allum Green, and Mr. John Everett of Colbury, both hunted regularly.

Then there was Lord Londesborough, who lived at Northerwood during the winter months, and often came out; but he was very short-sighted, and was obliged to have a pilot who rode in front of him. Lord Eslington (who afterwards became Earl of Ravensworth) lived somewhere on the south side of the country and was a keen sportsman. At one time I used to see Lord Percy (now Duke of Northumberland) out occasionally. There was a funny little man called Mudge who lived at Brockenhurst and trotted about on a white pony long after he was ninety; I think he had once been a Clerk in some Government office and was given a pension, which he certainly enjoyed to the utmost, for he lived to an immense age.

The Secretary to the Hunt was Captain Martin Powell, at that time Adjutant of the Hampshire Yeomanry, and formerly of the Inniskilling Dragoons. Never was there a better Hunt Secretary. Nowadays he is Colonel Powell of Brooklands, Lyndhurst, probably the oldest member of the Hunt Club, a Forest fox-hunter all his life, and now, as ever, a courteous, kindly gentleman.

During the summer of 1875 the Yorkshire Hound Show was held at Driffield, and I was asked to act as Judge there, in company with that celebrated Devonian the Reverend Jack Russell; the other Judge was Mr. Hill, who kept a north-country pack. We all went to stay with Mr. James Hall at Scorborough in the East Riding; he was a famous Yorkshire M.F.H., having been Master of the Holderness Hunt for about thirty years. There was a jovial party there, amongst whom I remember Lord Feversham, Sir Watkin Wynn, the Rev. Cecil Legard, and many others. In the showyard during that afternoon Jack Russell came over to me and, in what perhaps he thought was a whisper, said, in very audible tones, "I say, Graham, if you and I are going to stay at Bramham for next Sunday we had better give George Fox one of these prizes, or we shall never hear the last of it." His ideas of justice and merit were the cause of much laughter among the spectators. However, we did go to Bramham, and on the following

Hound Show at Peterborough

Sunday morning he gave us an excellent sermon, when it struck me that he was better in the pulpit that on the flags. Perhaps in Devonshire he may not have been accustomed to foxhounds of very high quality; anyhow, he did not strike me as exactly a good judge of hounds. All this took place long before the Peterborough Shows were established; though later on I often judged there for many years. Some of the best judges I met with in those days were the late Lord Willoughby de Broke, Sir Herbert Langham, Rev. Cecil Legard, Mr. Austin Mackenzie, and especially so was Captain Robert Arkwright, who had a successful career as Master and Huntsman of the Oakley Hounds from 1850 to 1885; I think he understood the whole game as well as anyone I ever knew.

After my first season Jack Goddard left to go to the Blankney, and Charley Hawtin came to me in his place. We began my second season on the 3rd September 1875 and finished on the 25th April; hunted eighty-nine days, and killed forty-seven foxes. All through that winter we had a succession of good sport, and although it was wild, cold weather and stopped twelve days by snow, it was about the best season I had down there. The only sad part of it was the death of my kennelman, William Andrews, a very good fellow.

The following was one of our good gallops in my second season: On the 16th November 1875 met at Lyndhurst Road Station. There was a large gathering of the hunt, it being a very fine morning. We went first to Deer Leap Enclosure, which was blank; then to Buscots, where a fox was on foot immediately. We ran him hard through Irons Hill and away over the open; turning to the right he pointed for Pond Head, and on nearly to the Brockenhurst Road, where he was headed and turned back across to the rifle-butts, and we killed him by the police station near Bolton's Bench, after about thirty-five minutes, and a capital pace all the time. The fox was a well-known customer (nicknamed "Dr. Kenealy") which had afforded many a run in Mr. Standish's time, but on this occasion twenty-two and a half couple of the "Fast Ladies" were too much for the old stager, whose brush I gave to the Hon. Francis Denison (son of Lord Londesborough); on a very fast pony he rode well, and saw the end of this sharp gallop.

I think the best day I ever had in the Forest, or anywhere else, was on the 14th February 1876, advertised at Brockenhurst Bridge at eleven. Snow was falling heavily, and a lot of it on the ground early in the morning. I never dreamed

FOX-HUNTING RECOLLECTIONS 69

there could be any hunting at all that day, and I stopped the hounds going on; but about twelve o'clock there was a bit of a change and I got to the meet at 1.30, and found nearly everybody had gone home except half a dozen, one of whom was Sir Claude de Crespigny. The snow was going fast and I was persuaded to draw, so we trotted down to Mr. Morant's coverts at Brockenhurst Park, where, to my surprise, we found directly and raced away to Boldre; then by Stockley, Frame, Pigbush, and back through the big Enclosures at Woodfidley and Denny, running the rides the whole way, and caught him close to Denny Lodge, about fifty-five minutes; such a scent, and they ran as if they were tied to him for the whole way. I never saw anything so fast before or since. Sir Claude and I were the only two at the finish, and he helped me to get the hounds back to the kennels, for both the whippers-in were lost, and so was everybody else.

Although this was far the best thing of the season, I had some regret about what happened, for I felt that if in spite of the snow I had gone to the meet an hour sooner (as I ought to have done) probably most of my field would have shared the sport. Soon afterwards we had another good day in the same part of the country, and the following account appeared in *Land*

and *Water* from the pen of "Cerise," a writer well known at that time :—

"On Saturday, March 11th, the meet was at New Park. Sir Reginald Graham has again shown us grand sport with a Brockenhurst fox, this time with the dog pack. After a longish draw, not finding till three o'clock, a splendid fox went away from New Copse, through Perry Wood, taking a good line for Brockenhurst Manor, but, for reasons best known to himself, turned sharp to the right across the railway, to Whitley, circling back through New Copse, Lady Cross, Frame, and Hawk Hill, on to Beaulieu Heath, heading right away for Norley, across Norley Farm, on to the Heath again, the hounds rolling over their fox dead beat in the open, within fifty yards of Norley Wood. The run lasted one hour and a half, with hardly a check. The country was terribly heavy, and the pace from Hawk Hill very fast—in fact, I think, quite as severe as our run from Brockenhurst on February 14th with the 'ladies,' when we killed near Denny Lodge. Out of a field of about thirty, only seven were up at the finish, namely, the Master, Lord Henry Scott, M.P., Sir Claude de Crespigny, Messrs. Powell-Montgomery, Duplessis, Emms, and the second whip. Since the melancholy death of his kennel huntsman, Sir Reginald is only able to take out one whip, Charles Hawtin, temporarily doing duty at the kennels. At our Hunt meeting to-day (14th), to the great satisfaction of the whole Hunt, Sir Reginald expressed his willingness to continue hunting the country."

Up to 1876 I had resided in my bachelor days at Jessamine Cottage, Lyndhurst, but the 24th of July in that year was the commencement of a happy life for me in double harness. We moved that summer to Fritham Lodge, two or three miles north of Stony Cross, a charming spot on high ground, with views all over the Forest.

This was my third season, and I began it with Charley Hawtin, and Walter Primmer came as second whip. I could not have been better whipped-in to than I was by those two. It was a very wet winter with constant rain, which always seemed to suit the Forest. We began on the 11th September and finished on the 27th April, and killed fifty-four foxes, the most I caught while in the New Forest.

The next season of 1877-78 began badly, as poor Charley Hawtin had recently died after a short illness. He was an immense loss, such a nice fellow, and as a huntsman he had a voice and a manner with hounds such as one seldom sees many times in one's life. He had been huntsman to Lord Henry Bentinck when only twenty-three years of age, and made a great name in the

Burton country for some time; but he had a bad fall and was never quite the same afterwards. Still, when he came to me in 1875 he was all right for a couple of years until his last illness. He was buried at Emery Down Churchyard, where his tombstone shows that he was only thirty-eight years of age when he died. Poor fellow, I never liked any hunt servant quite so well as him.

That same year Mr. Henry Compton of Minstead Manor also died, deeply regretted by everyone who knew him. I think he was about sixty-four, and I never knew a more hospitable friend.

About the same time died also George Cooper, the Crown Keeper at Bolderwood, a fine old fellow of seventy years of age, who had passed his life in the Forest and was much appreciated. These three sad events were a great blow, and I felt that hunting the country would never be quite the same to me without them.

In the place of Charley Hawtin I engaged Alfred Mandeville (I forget where he came from), a hard fellow who could stand any amount of work, and with his help we killed forty-seven foxes after a very good season, which ended on the 11th April 1878.

During that winter one of our good days was

FOX-HUNTING RECOLLECTIONS

described by the local papers in the following account signed "Sirius":

"6th November 1877. The New Forest Foxhounds.—Red-letter days have been rare, if not altogether unknown, with any packs of foxhounds thus far in this somewhat remarkable, or rather unremarkable, season. The run with the New Forest, of which I am now going to endeavour to give a description, if it did not occur on a day which deserves the name of a red-letter one, must at least be considered as extraordinary in more senses than one, even if we eliminate the sensational element from it altogether. Let me first point out that the New Forest Foxhounds are kept at Furzey Lawn, near Lyndhurst, Hampshire, and that the Master is Sir Reginald Graham, who has for his whips Alfred Mandeville and Walter Primmer. The nearest towns of approach for intending visitors, of whom it is unreasonable to expect there will be many after reading of this run, are Southampton, Lymington, and Ringwood, for the N. F. H. or New Forest Foxhounds.

"The meet was at the Vine Inn at Ower, when, after time allowed for stragglers, and those who have not learned the maxim concerning the early bird and the worm, to join the rendezvous, the order was given for a fast move for Embley. There a find was soon effected, the difficulty of discovering Reynard's whereabouts being surmountable, even by human nostrils, so glorious a scenting morning was it. This fox proved a right gallant one, and worthy of the famous pack at his brush. The coverts at Embley are extensive, and the grounds around corresponding, so the fox had plenty of tactics for trial before a permanent vacation of his domains. The scent was so hot, however, and he was raced so hard and persistently up and down his happy hunting-grounds, that he made occasional dashes out by way of feinting with his foes. First of all he made out on the side towards Romsey, and, finding that no go, he tried another similar venture towards Wellow. Home quarters, however, had now become much too warm for comfort, and Charley discovered that Embley was no longer for him a peaceful abiding place. His next bolt was across the lane and over the fields towards Pauncefote Farm. Thence he turned to the left down through the covert over the Salisbury Road to Greenhill, and down into the meadows as if steeplechasing to the Old Abbey Church at Romsey. Here a mob of fellows, who behaved as though they had never seen a real fox before in their lives, and who, as Mr. Carter remarks in a provinicial paper, 'must have fancied it was some wild foreign animal just escaped from Bostock and Wombwell's menagerie,' by their shouting and yelling turned him away again to the left. The point of the fox was evidently Romsey Abbey, but the hullabaloo caused another diversion, and the hounds now raced him fast and furiously the whole way up the meadows to Greatbridge, and pulled him down in fine style in the field adjoining Timsbury Mill. The finish was seen by very few of the well-appointed sportsmen of the morning, and the pace and country were all too trying for any but the most daring and the best mounted. In fact, beyond the Master and the whips, the field was reduced to a respectable unit, in the person of Mr. S. Carter of Totton, who claims the credit, and deserves it, of having seen the whole run. As for the rest, they had been shaken off for miles before the finish, and so distanced must they have been, that none of them came to the ' Whoohoop ' even after the fox was broken up.

" In this run with the New Forest no hounds could possibly have stuck more gamely to their fox, and, considering the nature of the country, very few could have gone faster. Though the scent was admittedly of a burning sort, yet it must be remembered that six or seven roads were crossed, a species of hunting which always tries hounds very much, and sometimes causes them to turn up the game altogether, unless there are a few staunch good-nosed ones among their number. It may be easily understood from this how it was that the field were so outrageously ' out of the hunt.' No doubt, however, many a neighbouring Hampshire man ' thinks himself accursed and holds his manhood cheap ' to reflect that he was not there to see something, however little, of this run from Embley, which unquestionably is likely to be talked about for many a day to come, or at all events until its fame shall have been eclipsed by a longer and more glorious one. It is but common justice to say that Sir R. Graham was with his hounds everywhere, and that he handled them in a most judicious and masterly manner. I hope that, notwithstanding an avoidance of anything like undue laudation or triumphant cracking of the descriptive whip, I have at least rescued this run of the New Forest Fox Hounds from total oblivion, and raised it out of the ruck of provinical records."— "SIRIUS."

I can remember a famous day on Thursday, 24th January 1878. Lord Percy was staying with me to have a look at the north of the country, which he had never seen, and I mounted him on a bay mare called Gelatine. We met at the Royal Oak, Fritham, with sixteen couple of doghounds; went first to Islands Thorns, a large enclosure which was full of deer that morning. They gave us some trouble, but I got the hounds together and trotted off a couple of miles to some gorse outside Sloden. An old fox was off like a shot, and we raced him at a rattling pace over the open heath for thirty-three minutes, and caught him between Goreley and Fordingbridge. It was a terrific pace, and when Mr. Bradburne got up to us he sang out to me, "Wherever you go, all your life you will never see such a gallop as that again." We found another fox in the afternoon at Hasley, but the scent had changed since the morning, and we lost him at Broomy Lodge.

At the end of this season I gave up the country and sold my hounds; the bitch pack went to my successor, Mr. George Meyrick of Hinton Admiral; the doghounds went partly to Lord Spencer, who was Master of the Pytchley, and partly to Lord Howth, who then kept the hounds at Pau.

In looking back to those times I should be inclined to say that if a man only "hunts to ride," he had better never go near the New Forest, but if, on the contrary, he "rides to hunt," then there is no limit to his enjoyment.

I have never seen any country where at times hounds ran harder than in the Forest: this was by no means an every-day occurrence. In the autumn the scent is often very moderate, and especially so when the leaf is falling; but when that is quite over, matters begin to improve, and from January to May — sometimes when the country is almost under water, or sometimes when the ground is as hard as iron—I have seen many days on which hounds can race from morning till night, especially with a straight fox who runs the rides in the enclosures and the tracks on the open heath. Those are the days to ascertain whether your hounds have got drive or not, and to my mind they are not of much use without it.

I have nothing but the most pleasant recollections of those happy hunting-grounds in the New Forest, and in spite of "Time who steals our hours away," my thoughts can still linger in a vision of those delightful spring mornings when I drew Matley Bog, and did not draw in vain.

CHAPTER VI

THE TEDWORTH HUNT

THE history of the Tedworth Country is inseparable from the name of Thomas Assheton Smith, who founded the Hunt and was Master from 1826 until he died in 1858. That celebrated sportsman, after a famous career from 1806 to 1824 as Master of the Quorn and Burton, returned to Hampshire to form a local hunt in his county, and to pass an old age in a country where he could still gallop after his own hounds.

Most of the Tedworth Country is composed of downs and light wold land, with but little fencing, which stretches for miles and miles; but there is a narrow strip on the north-west corner called the Pewsey Vale, while on the north there is an immense tract of lowlands which includes Savernake Forest. There are extensive woodlands towards the east, and on the south side a wild district surrounding the Danebury training-ground. What a difficult game to play Mr. T. A. Smith must have had when he first started with some draft hounds from Sir Richard Sutton, with which he commenced at Penton

Lodge in 1826. It sounds so surprising that any man who had passed most of his life in Leicestershire should have cared to undertake the conversion of such a territory into a hunting country.

His first difficulty was with his father, an irascible old gentleman who immediately warned his son off the Tedworth coverts. He did not, however, live long enough to cause him permanent annoyance, for on his death in 1828 the M.F.H. removed his establishment to Tedworth House, and took possession of the family estates both in Hampshire and in Wales.

In the huge woodlands of Doles Faccombe and Wherwell he set to work in earnest by having rides cut through them, so that he and his hunt servants could reach the hounds when drawing those woods. What labour he must have employed and what money he must have spent in carrying through such undertakings !

There was also the immense tract named Collingbourn Woods, of at least 1500 acres. A tradition has been handed down that in these woodlands Mr. Smith was in the habit of ordering bonfires to be lit to induce the foxes to fly ; certainly these woods were the key to the whole country, and in my time I used to rent them, as well as Southgrove, entirely for the preservation of foxes.

MR. THOMAS ASSHETON SMITH
1856

There was one bit of blue in the horizon; this was the immense expanse of Salisbury Plain, with its wide stretch of turf, which, with the bit of vale round Southgrove, formed the best part of the country, dotted with patches of gorse which mostly held a fox or two.

The Squire began by hunting four days a week himself in the best parts, and at the same time he sent his huntsman with another pack every Wednesday into Wherwell Wood, and every Saturday to some of the other great woodlands. At first Dick Burton was his huntsman, and after that old George Carter, who came to Tedworth in 1842 with a pack of hounds which Mr. Assheton Smith bought from the Duke of Grafton of that day. The soil on the downs was of cold and chalky nature, and perhaps it is safe to say of the Tedworth that you can either run fast over it or cannot run at all. Close at your fox on a favourable day you may perhaps race him from find to finish, and in a spin over the downs it often happens that you can see him all the way as he rises hill after hill of the undulating sheep-walks until the hounds get hold of him, but this is not every day. When the land is cold and hard and there is no scent upon the downs, then it is difficult to get a gallop. A good general idea of the open Tedworth Hills may be obtained from the summit of Beacon Hill, some few miles from the kennels. Let your eye wander over the sweeping undulations as far as you can see, and you will liken it to the unbroken billows of the ocean—mile upon mile of unruffled surface, with nothing to break the scene or hide the view; the downs dotted with sheep, and an occasional turnip-field or small plantation just show themselves here and there; it is all wild and picturesque beyond words.

I can actually remember Mr. Assheton Smith, as when, quartered at Winchester Barracks in 1857, he invited me over to stay at Tedworth, and I recollect hunting with his hounds one day when they met at Southgrove, which was considered about the best fixture in the hunt. Little did I think then, that some two-and-twenty years later on I should become the Tedworth M.F.H. instead of him.

At the time I speak of, his iron frame was rapidly giving way and the lamp was nearly out, for in August 1858 he died at Vaenol, his place in Wales, after a lingering illness. Like many another Master of Hounds of those days, his lot was cast in that period of hunting history probably the most conducive to sport. Pheasants and game-preserving were not then carried to

FOX-HUNTING RECOLLECTIONS 83

the extent of the present day; that method of barbarism, barbed wire, was actually unknown; countries were not gridironed by railways; and the enormous crowds which are nowadays to be found in any fashionable hunt, had then scarcely commenced to show themselves to the extent existing at the present time.

After the Squire's death in 1858 his widow presented the hounds to a Hunt Committee, with the 2nd Marquis of Ailesbury as the fountain-head. They carried on matters until he died in 1878, when there was some difficulty about the Hunt affairs, with the result that the Mastership was offered to me and I took over the country in 1879. At the same time I took a three years' lease of Netheravon House from Sir Michael Hicks-Beach, M.P., a very attractive place, with excellent trout-fishing in the river Avon, which ran under the windows.

The kennels were in Tedworth Park, not far from Tedworth House, which stands exactly on the boundary-line between Hampshire and Wiltshire. I found about fifty couples there, and the doghounds were rather on the large side. Jack Fricker was the huntsman, and had been at Tedworth all his life. The two whippers-in were John Bevan and Jack Thatcher. I engaged them all, and took over everything as it stood except the hunt horses, as I preferred to start with a fresh stud of my own.

We began cub-hunting on the 18th September, and during that season of 1879 and 1880 we hunted ninety-four days and killed eighty-two foxes up to 17th April, but we were stopped by frost twenty-nine days, and it was only a moderate season. We had two or three good points, however, one of them on the 24th November, a straight eight-and-a-half-mile point from Fargo to Wylye, and killed. At the same time another fox went away from Fargo with only a whipper-in and a few couples who caught him after a scurry over the downs. This was a very good day's sport, and the hounds killed four foxes during that day. On the 5th January there was a nine-mile point, with a fox from Round Down, near Everley, and we killed him in the middle of the West Woods. That morning we also had a sharp gallop with a fox from Pewsey gorse, and caught him at Upavon after twenty-five minutes.

My agreement with the country was to hunt four days a week, but I generally found enough hounds to make up a mixed pack, which I hunted myself on a bye-day, either Wednesday or Friday, and on these occasions Jack Fricker did not come out.

Some of the cub-hunting was delightful in

FOX-HUNTING RECOLLECTIONS 85

Savernake Forest, as the Lord Ailesbury of that day (this was the 3rd Marquis of Ailesbury) allowed me to take the hounds and horses to the Tottenham kennels at Savernake. Here they stayed for two or three weeks in the autumn, and we always found plenty of cubs to hunt.

The Saturday fixtures were generally Doles Wood or Faccombe Wood, an enormous tract of woodland on the east side of the country, surrounded by hills with arable land and endless flints; the consequence was that on those days the hounds often had their feet cut, which caused a deal of trouble in the kennel.

No one could say that the Tedworth was a really good fox-hunting country, or indeed a good scenting country, but I think it was one of the best for foxes that I have ever known. You could find them everywhere, and the farmers were one and all fox-hunters, and with them Jack Fricker was quite an idol for thirty or forty years—a good servant and a very honest man, patient and persevering in the field; but I always thought he might have made a better huntsman if he had been away a little into other countries early in life, instead of passing the whole of his career at Tedworth. There were, nevertheless, one or two points in which he was quite unequalled; he could make his hounds at any hour of the day draw the thickest gorses with more dash and determination than any professional I ever saw; and another thing, he always had them steady from riot. I have seen a hundred hares before the pack when puzzling out a cold line on the chalky hills, but no hound of his would ever look at a hare under any circumstances, not even in the wildest weather.

An unwelcome feature in this country were the dense fogs, which often came on suddenly without a minute's warning, and I remember that many of the field used to carry small compasses in their pockets. A great friend of mine, Mr. Godfrey Webb, was staying with me at Netheravon; he was well known in London life but not much accustomed to the chase. I persuaded him to have a day's hunting on a steady old horse of mine named Mortimer. In the afternoon of that day, when the sport was nearly over, we suddenly found ourselves in a fog and separated from my friend, who did not make his appearance at our house until late that evening. He then told a pathetic story of the sudden darkness which had come on about four o'clock, how he finished his last sandwich, how he drained the remnant of his flask, how he smoked his last cigar, and then resigned himself to his impending fate in the open air until day-

FOX-HUNTING RECOLLECTIONS 87

light. Happily for him, however, the sound of the dinner bell at Netheravon reached the ears of old Mortimer, who quickened his steps, and not long afterwards found his way in the dark to his own stables. As we came out from the dining-room about nine that evening, Godfrey Webb walked into the hall, and all ended well.

The next season of 1880 and 1881 was a hard winter; we were stopped by frost many days, and only killed sixty-nine foxes. During part of the time I was laid up with a severe attack of sciatica, the result of wading in the river when fishing the previous autumn, and consequently I missed a good many days' hunting.

The following season of 1881 and 1882 was very open; we were only stopped one day by frost and one day by fog, and killed seventy-eight foxes. In the spring of that year, 1882, I asked the Duke of Beaufort to bring his pack over to have an invitation day in the Tedworth country. It was a very long way for them to come by road, and it was not a success, as it turned out a wild windy day and a shocking bad scent. I remember a large party of sportsmen came with the Duke from Badminton, and among them was Lord Waterford, the 5th Marquis, who at that time had just been forced to relinquish hunting the Curraghmore Country in

Ireland owing to the proceedings of the Land League. For a few seasons after this he hunted in England, but when out with the Cottesmore in the spring of 1885 he had a very bad fall which injured his spine, crippled him for the rest of his life, and he died in 1895. Sad to think of all the sufferings which he endured in his latter years. Such a fine gallant fellow, and such a splendid fox-hunter!

Among my friends and supporters was old Sir John Kelk, who had just bought the Tedworth Estate, had built a house for himself in Grosvenor Square, and had been created a Baronet. He was very kind and hospitable, and gave me the free use of the kennels and stables at Tedworth; but he did not live long to enjoy his prosperity, and died a few years later. Then at Wilbury there was the Hon. Percy Wyndham (who afterwards succeeded me in the Mastership of the Hounds); he, his wife, sons, and daughters all hunted regularly, and were a very popular family.

At Conholt Park lived Lady Charles Wellesley; she was an excellent preserver of foxes on that estate. Her two sons, Henry and Arthur, were in the Grenadier Guards, and keen foxhunters. Later in life they both became Dukes of Wellington. Then from Amesbury came Sir

LORD ALGERNON ST. MAUR
Afterwards 14th Duke of Somerset

Edmund Antrobus, who was a constant attendant, and at that time probably about the oldest Member of the Hunt. Everley belonged to Sir John Astley (so well known as " the Mate "), who sometimes had a day with us; but he cared more for the turf than the chase, and the place was let to Mr. C. J. Curtis, who took it chiefly for shooting, but at the same time was the best of fox preservers.

At Wilcot Manor House there lived at that time Lord Algernon St. Maur, who afterwards became the 14th Duke of Somerset; he and his four sons were out every day, and they all delighted in hunting with the Tedworth. Lord Algernon had been formerly in the " Blues " (where he was known by the nickname of " Mousey "); a light weight, he always rode thoroughbred horses which could gallop, and when hounds were running nothing could restrain his ardour. Wherever he was, it was impossible to resist the charm of his old-fashioned courtesy and kindly nature; no wonder he was beloved by all who knew him. In former times he was often to be found in Hyde Park or at Tattersall's, arm in arm with his inseparable companions, Mr. George Lane Fox and the Earl of Macclesfield. During the sixties and seventies this trio was known as the " Ancient Critics," for no horse or carriage in London could escape their observation or their verdict. Lord Algernon was a most excellent coachman, and in early life passed much of his time in driving many of the Stage-Coaches of those days; he lived to a great age, and was actually driving a team on the day he died. I had known him intimately all my life, and had a very great regard for him.

Then there was Sir William Humphery, who lived at Penton House; and his constant friend, Mr. Bulwer, Q.C., from whom I bought a charming skewbald mare with a coat like satin, called Columbine, for which I gave him £80. I should have kept her much longer than I did, but Lord Londesborough gave me no peace until I let him have her for, I think, £120, as he wanted a leader for his London team. Then there was Mr. Stephen Butler of Stitcombe, and Mr. William Hayward of Wilsford, Mr. Fowle of Chute Lodge, Mr. Powell of Easton; Sir Michael Hicks-Beach who came now and then to stay at Netheravon for a day or two, and Sir Claude de Crespigny, who lived at Durrington, a man of iron nerve who regarded locked railway gates and sheep-hurdles with equal indifference. Also two or three well-known fox-hunting parsons, such as the Rev. W. H. Awdrey of Ludgershall, and the Rev. J. H. Gale of Milton, with a loud voice and rather abrupt manner; I think they used to call him " Rude Boreas."

My Hunt Secretaries were Mr. Stephen Allen of Eastover and Mr. Thomas Lamb of Andover; but previous to my era Mr. Brewer of Garlogs, near Stockbridge, had been from time immemorial the secretary to the Hunt Committee, a man of enormous size, who was a Master in Chancery, and went by the name of Master Brewer, partly because of his Chancery designation, and partly because he was rather apt to assume when he could the title of Master of the Hounds, an honour to which he had no right. One day when hunting on the downs, most of the field, who had lost the hounds, saw on the horizon an object in red; somebody cried out, " There's old Brewer going over the hill; the hounds can't be far off." After galloping a mile or two in hot pursuit they discovered that this object was an immense red water-butt which they had mistaken for the ample proportions of Master Brewer; but his shoulders were broad enough to carry most of the blame which was sometimes attributed to him.

I recollect inviting a Swedish " masseur " named Bramberg to come from London to stay with me for some hunting; a young man who had been very attentive to me during my sciatica troubles. He had been at one time in the Swedish Artillery, and I found he could ride pretty well, though naturally he was not accustomed to going out hunting. I mounted him on a white horse of mine called the Ghost, a very safe conveyance. The first day the meet was a long way off and he was not in the best of condition, but his enthusiasm was enormous and he enjoyed himself immensely. At the end of a long hard day we found ourselves about fifteen miles from home with a dreary ride over the hills before us. I noticed my friend apparently rather exhausted, and as we started on our homeward journey he cried out to me, "Oh, if I only knew where to get a glass of Swedish Punch!" To his dismay I had to break it to him that Swedish Punch was a beverage unknown to the English people, and that no public-house lay within many miles of our homeward route. Our progress was slow, and the only way by which I could get him along at all was the oft-repeated promise that, if we ever did fetch home, he should quench his thirst to his heart's content. Our goal was at last reached, but never in my life did I see a couple so completely done as the "Ghost" and the "Swede."

At the end of the first season we had a capital week, considering it was the month of April. On the 6th we met at Savernake Ruins; found in Birch Copse; ran through Henswood to Chisbury, and lost. Drew Savernake Wood; found directly; ran through Puthall and Henswood to Birch Copse, by Tottenham House, and round the Forest to the Eight Walks, and back to the Monument, and killed; one hour and twenty minutes' good forest hunting.

April 10. Collingbourn Shears.—Found in the Clay-pits, and ran a ring round the Rags, through Shaw Copse, back through the Rags and Heath Copse to Scots Poor, by Jubilee Clump, through Chantry; forced him through the wood and out by Crawlboy's Farm, over Ludgershall Common, through Mr. Young's plantation to the top of Tedworth Hill, where there were two lines, and he beat us. Found again on Sidbury Hill, and ran very fast through Dunch Hill to Shipton, where a false hallo took us back to Tedworth, and we were obliged to give it up. With a little luck this would have been a good day, as it was one of the very few this season on which hounds could really push their fox along.

April 13. Southgrove.—Two hallos directly hounds were put into covert. Went away towards Grafton over the heavy ploughs nearly to Wexcombe; over Fair Mile, where he turned to the right and skirted Heath Copse, and so through the Rags and Shaw Copse, Chantry, through Jubilee Clump to Scots Poor, where he was headed and lay down in Hippenscombe Gorse, and they killed him, an old dog-fox; time, 1 hour 23 minutes. A real good sporting run. Found again in Grafton Park a fox which at first ran through all the farm buildings he could find in his line, then through Wexcombe, and on to Tedcombe Hill, where he lay down in a pit till the hounds fairly worked up to him, and catching a view they rolled him over in the open within half a mile of the big woods; time, thirty-two minutes. This brought us up to forty-one brace, the total for that season of 1879-80.

We began again, as usual, the next autumn, and had a good November, some of them very fair days.

On Monday the 15th, 1880, we met at Netheravon House, where we then lived during the winter months. A large field turned up, amongst whom were Lord Algernon St. Maur, Lord Lawrence, Lord Wiltshire, Sir William Humphery, Sir Edmund Antrobus, Hon. Percy Wyndham, M.P., Mrs. and Miss Wyndham, and many others.

At half-past eleven the hounds moved off to draw one of the coverts which I rented sloping to the river Avon, and instantly a brace of foxes were on foot; one went away over the park with the hounds very handy to him; raced over the water meadows up to Fittleton village, then he set his head straight over the downs until turned by a team of horses at work, and was caught in the open close to the village of Upavon. The pace was pretty good, distance five miles, and time thirty-five minutes.

Found another fox almost directly in a turnip-field; gave him a good dusting for twenty-five minutes, and lost him in a storm near Wilsford.

We then trotted off a couple of miles to draw Chirton Gorse, a capital covert on the hills, but a deluge of rain brought matters to a close for this day; the doghounds were out (nineteen couples), and I thought they did very well in rather wild weather.

Monday, Nov. 29.—Met at Wilbury, always a favourite down meet, especially of late years, since the old place became the residence of the Hon. Percy Wyndham, M.P., a kind and hospitable friend to all around. A fine still morning, and eighteen couples of bitches stood in the park until 11.30, where some seventy horsemen and half a dozen ladies had assembled. Everyone was of course pleased to see Lady Graham again on horseback with the hounds, her first appearance, this season. Trotted off a mile to draw the Warren; found, and away over the open through the Park to the wood near the house; some puzzling work among the hares there; got up to him, and killed. Time about thirty minutes. Moved away a couple of miles to Tower Hill; three or four foxes on foot instantly, one of whom was soon offered up. Whistled away after another down the belt of trees to the South-Western Railway; ran parallel to it for a mile, away to the right over the open downs, leaving Old Lodge to the left, and to ground in some gorse in the Roche Court direction; a sharp burst of about twenty-five minutes, rather spoilt by over-riding. I read the Riot Act decidedly, and without distinction of persons—not before it was wanted. On our way back the field were refreshed by Lord Lawrence at his residence, Old Lodge, and the hounds jogged on to Folly Hill; got up to a fox, and soon ran him to ground. Then over the railway to the Warren, and fastened on to another, who took them almost in view down to the Park; bustled him in the coverts there, and killed—twenty minutes—eating our last fox under Wilbury House windows, on precisely the same spot as the first fox of the morning. Hounds started

FOX-HUNTING RECOLLECTIONS

home at four; during the day had six foxes on foot and killed three.

Tuesday, Nov. 30, at Upavon Village.—Six red and about thirty black coats composed the field. A still morning; twenty couples of doghounds. Drew the osier bed near Rushall,—a brace of foxes at home. Away directly with one who swam the river, and over the meadows up to Wood Bridge; across the high road pointing straight through the Pewsey Vale, by Manningford, over the fields to the Great Western Railway, up the line and on to Wilcot, leaving Lord A. St. Maur's place to the left, over the Canal Bridge by Stowell to Draycott, and away over the heavy fields towards Oare Hill; then to the left, and up the hillside through Coker Wood, over the open downs to the Wans Dyke, close to Hewitt's Gorse, where the fox lay down in a sheep-fold. Got a view and rolled her over—a wiry old vixen as stiff as a poker. A hunting run of one hour and fifty minutes and an eight-mile point—a fact worth recording, as they ran some twelve miles. A sporting hunt enjoyable to those who care to see a dog pack do their work and throw their tongues really well. The Pewsey Vale was never much deeper, and thus some over-eager horsemen were nicely handicapped. The vast extent of the Tedworth country is here illustrated by the fact that where we killed our fox this day is nearly thirty miles north of the spot on which a similar event took place the previous afternoon.

The most curious finish to a fox hunt that I ever witnessed was killing a fox in the racquet-court at Marlborough College on 31st January 1882, of which the following account appeared in a Wiltshire newspaper :—

"The Tedworth Hounds had quite a holiday meet at Oare Hill on Tuesday. All who could get a 'mount' for the day turned out to enjoy the national pastime, and hundreds were scarcely less active on 'shank's mare.' Not only was the meet a large one, but the finish of the first run at Marlborough created no little excitement in the precincts of Marlborough College. The fox who sought refuge thither, was found in West Woods, the vast extent of which may be imagined when we say that 600 acres of the coppice belong to Sir Henry Meux alone. Reynard was forced from the woods, went to Gore Coppice, back again, then made for Granham, passed the house and turned sharp round to the White Horse down ; without stopping to admire the glorious panorama here visible of the town and downs to the north and east, our fox went at a cracking pace down the hill, crossed the river, and entered the College Master's garden. The pack was too close upon him for any stay, and desperately seeking shelter amid the haunts of men (for we may not presume that, with all the cunning of the tribe, a fox could be aware of the vacation) it bolted through the passage into the College court or quadrangle, crossed it, and sought shelter in the racquet-court. Here two young gentlemen were at play, and they were not a little astonished by the sudden entry of the fox, followed by the pursuing hounds, Sir Reginald Graham, Jack Fricker, and a large field. It did not take long to despatch him, and the next thing we saw was the head in the possession of Mr. C. M. Bull, who considers that it will, when preserved, form an interesting object in the College Museum, to which he intends presenting it. Another fox got up in the withy bed close to the chapel, but its career was short, for it was speedily chopped in the water meadow near Preshute House."

On the last day of this season, Tuesday, 21st March, we had a fair hunting run with a satisfactory finish. Met at Savernake ruins at twelve with the dog pack. After some forest hunting in the morning we went to Henswood and found a good straight fox, which we killed just outside the town of Hungerford; not much pace, but a six-mile point. This brought us up to a total of thirty-nine brace for the season of 1881–82.

We had a good bit over twenty-two miles back to Netheravon that evening, and it was my last day for ever in the Tedworth country.

About this time the force of circumstances induced me to go away to live in the North Riding of Yorkshire, and it was with very great regret I was obliged to resign the Mastership of the Tedworth Hunt.

I am told that nowadays Netheravon House is the headquarters of a Cavalry School, that the surrounding district is a mass of camps and huts, and that in some parts many miles of wire have appeared. I only speak of this from hearsay, as I have never again been in that district. Even now I like to think of the country as I once knew it in those old days, when in congenial company I found so much friendship and fox-hunting.

CHAPTER VII

THE HURWORTH HUNT

THE Hurworth country is partly in Durham and partly in Yorkshire, the River Tees dividing the northern from the southern portion. The Hunt appears to date a long way back, and was carried on for many years by the Wilkinsons of Neasham Abbey, a family of brothers whose names were Thomas, Lozelure, and Matthew. The Master in the early part of the last century was Thomas, and after his death the Hunt was continued by the two remaining brothers, whose names, according to the custom of the country, were curtailed into "Lozzy" and "Matty." The latter was both Master and Huntsman, and enjoyed much reputation as a sportsman, in fact he became a hero even in the eyes of "Nimrod," who in his "Yorkshire Tour" of 1827 wrote a great deal about him to the *Sporting Magazine* of that year. I will quote the description in "Nimrod's" own language:

"On Friday morning Mr. Flounders accompanied me to Croft Bridge to meet the Hurworth Hounds, which place was about eight miles from

Yarm. Our road to Croft also led us through the village of Hurworth, within a short distance of the Hurworth Kennel, and we overtook the hounds going to covert. They were accompanied only by Mr. Wilkinson and his whipper-in, and Mr. Flounders took this opportunity of introducing me to Mr. Wilkinson. I found him very much what I expected to find him: a well-fed Englishman, with a back as broad as those of three of our dandies put together; mounted on a finely shaped chestnut horse, looking very like a hunter to carry a heavy seventeen stone, which he had then on his back; with a keen eye in his head, and a very intelligent countenance—strong, to be sure, in the dialect of his county, but looking very much like a sportsman, and therefore claiming my respect.

"There was a very large field of sportsmen assembled at Croft Bridge on this day—amounting to at least one hundred, which is a very unusual circumstance with this pack. Mr. Lambton's hounds, however, were gone from Sedgefield, and Lord Darlington's were a long way off; so it was supplied by the gentlemen of those hunts, many of whom had come a long distance for the occasion. I am happy to add, some of them were well requited for their pains.

"We proceeded to draw Dinsdale Wood, a covert of some size and situated on a steep hanging bank. Before throwing in his hounds, Mr. Wilkinson did me the honour of asking me to accompany him into the wood and see him find his fox. This invitation I readily accepted, and so far I was most gratified. He found his fox almost instantly, and in very excellent style. His hallos were capital, and his ear unusually quick. This was not all. We had a very baffling fox on foot—very unwilling to break— and his turns were short and frequent. The pack and their Master, however, were quite a match for him, and for about five minutes the scene—witnessed only by ourselves—was enchanting. 'Have at him, Music, good bitch,' halloed Matty. 'By Jove, th'ast better gang away, for thou'lt die if thou don't. Have at him, Cruiser, old fellow, but thou'lt have his head in thy mouth before night.' Oh, that I could give his view-hallos on paper, but that can't be done. They were enough to raise a man from the dead.

"Mr. Wilkinson wished to see his hounds get well away with their fox, and therefore stood still and blew his horn ; but he should have ridden on, and blown his horn ; for when we got to the top of the covert, not a hound, except a few that were with us, could we get sight of. 'I know where they are gone,' said Mr. Wilkinson ; 'you must follow me, for we shall never get over that stell.' I did follow him, and he took me to an awkward ford ; but we might just as well have gone round by York. The hounds had a capital run of an hour, and killed their fox, but only in the presence of a chosen few, who were bold enough and fortunate enough to get well over this awkward stell—Billy Williamson, I believe, being the first to charge it. It was deep and rotten, and the change that was effected in the colour of the ci-devant white cords of those gentlemen who dropped short of it, plainly showed what sort of a bottom it had.

"Two things were now evident : I was quite sure they were in for a run, and I was quite sure I should see nothing of it unless let in by some lucky turn. I did not, however, quit my pilot ; but, strange to say, I rode for exactly one hour about fifty yards behind him, without ever hearing the tongue of a hound until within the last ten minutes. When we did get up to them, the thing was over, the whoo-hoop was only wanting. They had not tasted him, but he was dead beat, and in a few minutes more Matty had him by the brush. It must have been a beautiful run for those who saw it. The pace was excellent ; and the country very good indeed for the provincials.

"I had two reasons why I did not regret this wrong turn at first starting. First, I and my horse might have been planted in the stell ; and secondly, it was a great treat to me to see Matty Wilkinson and his chestnut horse get over, or I should rather say creep over, upwards of a hundred fences in the very masterly manner they both performed. He has ridden this horse three seasons without having had a fall from him ; and when I saw him creeping over his fences, which appeared nothing to him, whilst my

FOX-HUNTING RECOLLECTIONS 105

horse was flying over them, and afraid to touch a thorn, I almost envied his great weight. Certain, however, is it, that hunters carrying heavy men do walk into their fences in a most enviable manner, although, indeed, if they did not walk into them, they could never gallop across a deep country for an hour, and a hundred fences into the bargain.

"I really was much pleased with the scientific manner in which Mr. Wilkinson and his horse crossed the country in this hour's gallop. We exchanged but few words with one another—with the exception of his telling me he was too heavy for a huntsman, and an occasional lamentation of our ill-luck. Matty, however, once addressed his horse, and it had the desired effect. We came to a very awkward fence, a wide ditch from us, and no footing for our horses but among some strong stubs. 'Tak' time, lad,' said Matty. The lad did take time, and did it like a workman. Towards the end of our gallop we came to another still worse place. It was high and stiff and near to a tree. Matty rode up to it, and not liking it, stood looking at it. 'Shall I try and pull down those strong binders,' I said. 'No, no,' replied Matty, 'we'll gang at it,' and over he went at a good hard gallop. All his fences but this were taken either at a stand or in a walk.

"This certainly was a good run, and a good finish, and the brush was asked for by a gentleman (Mr. Dryden, I think) who had ridden well to the hounds. 'No, no,' said Matty, '"Nimrod" shall have the brush,' and it hangs up in my hall. It is quite evident I had no pretensions to it, therefore I considered it the greater compliment. We drew again, and three foxes all broke covert at the same moment; but we did nothing worth speaking of, although they tasted one of them.

"Matty, however, is the hero of my tale; and his character is described in a few words. He boasts of no scholastic education, no collegiate reading; neither does he appear to be much under the discipline of art. But of this he may be proud — he keeps a pack of foxhounds on perhaps smaller means to keep them with than almost any other man in England; and he is acknowledged by all to be as good a rough-and-ready sportsman as ever halloed to hound. He is likewise much esteemed amongst his neighbours as a kind-hearted man, a character, indeed, true sportsmen for the most part lay claim to and maintain.

"In everything relating to the passion for hunting, I should be inclined to say, Mr. Matthew Wilkinson may have his equal, but his superior would be difficult to produce. His attachment to his hounds is almost beyond belief, and nearly equals that of an old maid to her cat. He has always some of his favourites walking about his house; and to a bitch with whelps he will give as much as she can eat of a good sirloin of beef or leg of mutton from his own table. I had it on unquestionable authority that, although he keeps ten or twelve cows, the whelps in the spring have all the best milk, and nothing but a little sky-blue is allowed for the house. I was also informed that it has been his practice to keep a tame fox which would run about the house and buildings for the edification of the puppies as soon as they were able to follow him. He keeps but four hunters for himself and Tommy, and his stable system is this : His horses are never physicked, neither are they galloped in their exercise—having, as he observes, 'plenty of galloping when they hunt.'

"Death and its terrors kick the beam when put into the scale against Matty Wilkinson's passion for the chase. Although he cannot swim, no, not even a little, he has crossed that rapid and deep river, the Tees, at least forty times in his life after the hounds, and has had some hair-breadth escapes. Very soon after I was in his country, he was in the greatest danger of being drowned. He plunged into this stream when swelled with rain, and was unhorsed in the middle of it. Fortunately catching hold of one of the stirrups, his horse dragged him out, but I believe it was what he called 'a very near go.' When he had run his fox to ground he coolly laid himself down on his back, and held up his heels to enable the water to run out of his boots.

"I very much fear this gallant sportsman will, one of these days, change time for eternity in his attempts to cross this rapid river. Indeed, on his late escape, his brother Lozzy seriously admonished him of the impending danger; but all the notice taken of the salutary hint was—' My life is my own, and I suppose I may do what I like with it.'

"When Mr. Matthew Wilkinson's eldest brother was on his deathbed, he was asked by a friend for the fixtures for the forthcoming week. His reply was this: ' Why, Tommy is very ill, and if Tommy dies, we can't hunt till Monday; but if Tommy don't die, we shall hunt somewhere on Friday.' A brother sportsman died, and left Matty five pounds to purchase a black coat to his memory, Matty purchased a red one, thinking thereby that he had shown still greater respect to his departed friend.

"Mr. Matthew Wilkinson is esteemed a very superior huntsman as far as the working of his hounds is concerned, as also assisting them in recovering a scent. His great weight, however (full seventeen stones), precludes the possibility of his always being in his place; though everyone I conversed with agreed that, from his great knowledge of the country, and of the usual line of his foxes, he creeps up to his hounds, when at fault, much sooner than might be expected. This is the result of a quick eye and a good share of brains, with each of which Mr. W. is very well furnished. Of his management in the kennel I can say nothing; nor can I say much of the condition of his pack, any further than that their elbows were clean, and that is as much as can be generally said of hounds that work as hard as his do; but I thought the hounds themselves did credit to his judgment. They are fine slashing animals, with great power and bone, and are allowed to have as much hunt in them as their owner has zeal; and truly that is in abundance. Tattler, Cruiser, and Juggler would be an ornament to any pack. The subscription, I understand, amounts only to £175 per annum, which may, perhaps, with good management, find meal for the hounds, as the pack is small, only consisting of twenty-six couples of hunting hounds, and this year not more than four couples to come in.

"I have now done with Matthew Wilkinson and his hounds. Long may he live to enjoy his favourite sport; and when he is gone let his memory be cherished for the zeal he has shown in the noble science of fox-hunting."

Later on in the forties the name of Frank Coates appears as the huntsman with much local celebrity. After him, in the fifties, came Will Danby, who had seen service with both the Holderness and the York and Ainsty, but all this seems to have come to an end somewhere about the year 1860, when another generation of the old Wilkinson family became Master, with the well-known Mr. Thomas Parrington as huntsman finding his own horses.

This Squire Wilkinson, however, seems to have had but a short innings, as he died in 1861. About that date the second Duke of Cleveland was giving up his Raby country, and he offered some portion of it to the Hurworth, which enabled them to go out three days a week instead of two.

Mr. James Cookson of Neasham then succeeded as Master, and Mr. Parrington continued as huntsman with him until 1864, when he retired.

Sport seems to have risen to a high standard during Mr. Parrington's time, and from a diary still in his possession I extract in his own words the records of some of the best days he had:

" Tuesday, February 26th 1861.—Met at Hurworth; found a brace or leash of foxes in Mr. Wilkinson's cover at Neasham; chopped one instantly. At the same moment another broke away to Dinsdale Wood, with which we got away on pretty good terms. He left the wood a little west of the Asylum, and ran a ring at a good pace to Grey's Plantations, where presently several foxes were on foot and began to ring about in all directions, so stopped the hounds and trotted away to Mr. Surtees's Plantation. Found quickly; broke almost in view to the east, ran a ring nearly back to the Plantation, and then went straight away to the Fish Locks, where the hounds fairly chased down their fox in splendid style after a magnificent burst of twelve minutes; a fine old vixen-fox. Tried Bolton Park, then on to Mill Wood, where we unkennelled a fine old dog-fox; forced him away at a racing pace past Mr. Grace's to West Wood, thence to Pettly, and away to Mr. Surtees's Plantations; then a ring in the open, and back to the Plantations; then away to Bolton Park, on to opposite Girsby Village, where he crossed the Tees; then pointed for the Fish Locks, where, turning to the right, he went direct towards Long-Backed House, crossed Staindale, and away through Beverley Wood; then turned away to Allen's Plantations and down to the Tees west of Sockburn, was headed short back to Allen's Plantations, away for Eryholme; then turning past Brick House, ran again for the Tees; viewed him ere he reached the river, and ran into him in the stream after a most magnificent run of one hour and five minutes from Sockburn without a check; a fine old dog-fox, and $19\frac{1}{2}$ couples of hounds out, only one couple wanting at the last whoo-hoop. The fox we chopped in the morning proved to be the fox we had such a severe run with from Fighting Cocks on Saturday. A most capital day's sport, only eleven horsemen out of a very large field saw the finish.

"Saturday, 9th November 1861.—Met at High Worsall Toll Bar. Found in the Whin; broke at the north end away for Worsall Gills, which he left on his right, and running a ring over Worsall Moor brought us to Picton Plantations; right through, leaving Picton village on his right, and also Kirklevington Mill, ran direct to a drain near Yarm, which he found stopped; at this point the hounds had a moment's check, after running their fox for thirty minutes at a most terrific pace, and scattering the field all over the country.

Our fox struggled on to Scarfit Hill, where a lot of fresh foxes came to his rescue; the hounds divided and eventually we lost him. Found again in Worsall Gills; broke away past Fardenside, pointing for Girsby, then wheeled round and away as the crow flies to Worsall Toll Bar Cover, which he passed close by, running forward for Kirklevington, turned for Picton, and ran a ring back to the Toll Bar Cover (time to this point, forty minutes). Our fox now hung in the cover for nearly an hour; at last he was compelled to quit, and broke away to Mr. Waldy's Plantation, thence to Mourie Bank, along by the margin of the Tees to the railway at Yarm, then to the right of Kirklevington Lane, crossed the railway and pointed to Mr. Meynell's Woods; but, as he had not strength to jump the boundary wall, he turned back across the railway past the brickyards, where the hounds caught a view and ran into him on the edge of the Tees after a magnificent run of two hours and a quarter—a splendid old dog-fox. A fine crisp morning, and good scenting day; had nineteen couples of hounds out. Many of our field went home satisfied after the first run. There never was a better day's sport than this with hounds.

"Saturday, 1st February 1862.—Met at High Worsall Toll Bar. Found in the cover instanter, and away he went pointing for Picton Plantations, which he left on his right; then forward to Picton village and to the railway, which he did not cross, but ran parallel with it nearly to

FOX-HUNTING RECOLLECTIONS

Kirklevington drain; then turning he ran for the cover again at the Toll Bar, which he did not enter, however, but left it short to his left, and pointed for Worsall Gills; but swinging to the left he ran over Worsall Moor, crossed Staindale, and away, leaving Appleton Wiske on his right, to Welbury Village, which he left suddenly on his left, and turned away for Deighton; and still bending his course, he again crossed the Wiske, and running over the pasture in front of Hornby Grange he made the best of his way apparently for Beverley Wood, but strange to say he turned away from it when within half a field, and running for Smeaton Village, which he passed close on the east end, he again got to the Wiske and struggled on to near Hornby Grange, where he was killed after one of the best runs ever known in the Hurworth country. Of one hour and forty minutes very fast from end to end, and barring a slight check soon after he broke cover, there was no sobbing time afforded for anyone; consequently the horses were dreadfully beaten, and were left planted all over the country. The style in which the bitch pack did their work was most excellent; they ran with wonderful head from end to end, and only one hound (old Marigold) was wanting at the finish. I may particularly mention Timely Music and Dewdrop as always being in the van. Amongst the sportsmen who were lucky enough to be out to-day, I may say that Messrs. Cookson, Williamson, C. Simpson, and Garbutt went very well for the first twenty minutes, but at the end of an hour they were all more or less beaten. I was lucky enough to have a second horse, and, changing near Deighton, I managed to keep with the hounds to the finish. A remarkable fine old dog-fox; had eighteen couples out, including three doghounds. This run I now think the best I had during the four seasons I hunted the Hurworth.

" Thursday, 6th November 1863.—In spite of a very dense fog we threw off at noon in Blackman Cover; found directly; broke at the N.W. corner, and, running north a couple of fields, turned to the right across the turnpike road and away to Briar Flat Wood; then turned sharp back up the riverside and crossed to the Batts, ran their whole length, and then recrossed into Dalton Wood, and passing Dalton Village went to ground in a drain by the railway side after a clipping burst of twenty-four minutes, most of which was only seen by myself on account of the fog. After a good deal of delay in procuring a terrier the fox was bolted, and went away pointing for Clervaux Castle, which he left on the right, and then pointing for Halnaby, ran a ring back to the railway, and crossed the line running for Blackman Cover, which he ran past and crossed the road, going direct for Forty Acres; but after getting within a couple of hundred yards of the Cover, he suddenly changed his course, and wheeling round to the right he ran close past Blackman House and then away for

FOX-HUNTING RECOLLECTIONS 115

Cowton Plantations. Most unfortunately the hounds divided at the railway, one half running up the line and the other half crossing to the west, which I followed in order to get the hounds off the line, and we lost at Cowton Village. We afterwards discovered that the other half of the hounds with the run fox went straight up the railway to the earths near Cowton Station, where they ran their fox to ground. In their chase up the line they unluckily met a train, and one of them, Dainty, was run over and killed on the spot.

" This run from the drain to the point where the hounds divided, was exactly one hour and five minutes, and was undoubtedly first class from beginning to end. The pace was tremendous all the way, and only four of the field kept them in view, namely, the Master on his brown horse, Colonel Scurfield on Sambo, young Mr. Fowle of Northallerton on a chestnut horse, and myself on Lady Bennett, and never during the whole chase were we able to see more than seventy or one hundred yards ahead of us on account of the fog."

From 1865 to 1869 the Hurworth Master was Major Elwon (the owner of Plaudit); then again the same Mr. Cookson (a breeder of some famous racehorses, Mincemeat, Kettledrum, Dundee, and many others). In 1873 he retired in favour of Lord Castlereagh (the present

Marquis of Londonderry), who was M.F.H. for two seasons, with George Dodds as his huntsman; then Major Godman, formerly of the Carabiniers; then Mr. Cookson once more came to the rescue, and after him Mr. W. H. A. Wharton of Skelton Castle from 1884 to 1886, when he left to take the hounds in Cleveland.

For that position he was well adapted, as who could be more fitting as Master of the Cleveland Hunt than the Squire of Skelton Castle; and long may he continue to enjoy prosperity in that office.

In the spring of 1886 I took over the Hurworth and hunted the country five days a fortnight for two seasons; I found that I required more hounds, and Lord Lonsdale, who was at that time hunting the Blankney country, kindly let me purchase about eighteen couples of his beautiful Blankney bitches; they were of the same old sort which I had always liked so much, and I was very lucky to get hold of them, for they helped me to show sport in the famous Hurworth country.

Will Nicoll, from the Cleveland, came as Kennel Huntsman and first whip: a capital fellow to go out hunting with, and he did very well for me. William Rees, from the Wheatland, came as second whip, but in the following season

I got George Tongue from Earl Ferrers in his place, and he turned out a most useful fellow; nowadays he is huntsman to the Essex Union Hunt.

While with the Hurworth I had nothing but grey horses both for myself and the servants. Some people seem to think it such a difficult matter to collect a lot of hunters of one colour. I never could see why. Perhaps there might be a difficulty sometimes in providing the money to pay for them, but to find horses of the right colour was easy enough.

The Hurworth is bounded on the north by the South Durham; on the west by Lord Zetland and the Bedale; on the east by the Cleveland.

A vale of stiff clay with a certain amount of plough, but plenty of grass, especially in the Northallerton district, and on the whole I should call it a better scenting country than some of its neighbours. The Tees, the Leven, and the Wiske intersect the district, and although these rivers were no serious obstacle to the fox and a pack of hounds, they sometimes proved an impediment to those who followed the chase.

In my time there were some capital gorse coverts, notably, Fighting Cocks, Elton, and Farrer's Whin on the Durham side; then south of the Tees there were famous gorses at Welbury,

Deighton, Worsall, Trenholm, Stank, Winton, and Oliver's Whin.

I have known nothing more delightful in all my hunting career than some of those fast gallops from Welbury or Winton to the hills. The following account appeared in a Northallerton newspaper of one of the best runs which took place in my time:—

" On Thursday, 9th February 1888, had a bye-day at Sigston Bridge. The weather was all that could be desired. A small and select field met to enjoy the sport. First drew Sigston Wood; got on a drag at once; hunted slowly into Landmoth Wood, where a brace of foxes were on foot. We went away past Beacon Hill and Marigold Hill, across the Carrs to Spring Wood and on to Low Silton, where scent failed and he was lost. The hounds were then trotted away to Winton Whin, where they at once found Reynard at home. Without hesitating a moment he broke at the north-west corner of the covert as if for Welbury, with the hounds close at him, but quickly changing his course, he left Harlsey Castle to the left, over Mr. Raper's farm, crossed the Harlsey Road, through Bruncliffe Whins, away over the Thirsk and Yarm Road near where the old toll-bar stood, into Arncliffe Wood; the pace up to this point was terrific, the bitch pack fairly racing over this beautiful bit of country. Without stopping a moment they dashed up the big wood, and were for a short time lost to view. The horsemen taking the road up the wood past Mount Grace, had the good luck to find the hounds had come to a check near Lady Chapel, but the gallant Master (Sir R. Graham) being on the spot quickly, caught hold of his beautiful little ladies and, making a galloping cast to the left, hit off his fox.

" They then ran parallel with the Wood to the top of the Cliff, where they turned full east, racing over the open moor to Scarth Neck, over the Swainby and Osmotherley Road past Wild Goose Nest, skimming the enclosures like a flock of pigeons and topping the walls like greyhounds.

" Leaving Slapestones on the left they dashed into the valley over the stream into Thimbleby Wood, where this gallant fox saved his brush, or rather all that was left of it (for he was a bobtailed one), by going to ground in the Alum Works.

" Time from find to finish, fifty-five minutes, with only the slight check above named.

" Distance at least nine miles, and taking into consideration the nature of the country, particularly the latter part of it, this must be acknowledged as one of the fastest and best runs of the season."

This was a real good day, and no one rode better than the Rev. Charles Atkinson, at that time the Rector of Sigston, near Northallerton, a capital sportsman and often out with the Hurworth Hounds on that side of the country.

In the vicinity of Hurworth the Scurfield family have for long owned a considerable estate, on which their numerous coverts were well looked after, in fact they were " model lodging-houses " whence foxes were always forthcoming. Probably in these days there are many other coverts of equal note, but I only mention some of those which existed in former times.

There was not much woodland in the country, Beverley on the north and Cotcliffe on the south were the largest strongholds ; but on the south-east corner came the big woods of Thimbleby and Arncliffe, and it was hereabouts that the boundary was joined by the Bilsdale, a moorland hunt and a trencher-fed pack which had existed for ages. Sometimes they came on the line of a fox into the heart of the Hurworth Vale, and tradition had it that they were not very particular about what they did on these occasions. One of their Masters, Mr. Nicholas Spink of Bilsdale, ran a fox down to Welbury Whin, dug him out there, and took him away in a sack. This occurred when Lord Castlereagh was Master of the Hurworth, who at once wrote through his Hunt Secretary to remonstrate with the Bilsdale M.F.H. on his gross breach of hunting customs, which resulted

in a letter containing the following curt reply:
"We allus dig.—Nicholas Spink."

I will quote from my diary two or three of the good days which took place in my time:

"Tuesday, 15th March 1887.—Met at Great Burdon; sixteen couple of doghounds; snow on the ground and very cold; drew the quarry and found a brace; killed one and took the other by Fighting Cocks up to Foxhills in the South Durham country, and lost him there. Went back to draw Fighting Cocks; found directly, and away by Goose Pool and Burn Wood to Foxhills again, and back as hard as we could go to where we found him at Fighting Cocks. I saw the fox go into the covert apparently dead beat, but a heavy snow-storm came on and we never picked him up. It was snowing most of the day, and only three or four people out; the coldest day I ever remember.

"Saturday, 5th November 1887.—Met at Welbury; sixteen and a half couples of bitches; drew the Whin, four or five foxes there; ran one to ground in five minutes, then raced away with another towards the hills, where he turned back and we caught him at Rounton Grange; thirty-five minutes and a good gallop. Drew Deighton Whin blank, then to Appleton Spinney; a capital thirty minutes up to Staindale, and stopped them at dusk; a good many strangers came by rail from York.

"Tuesday, 27th March 1888.—Met at Long

Roofed House; seventeen couples of bitches; drew Worsall Whin; ran hard for thirty-five minutes and lost him at Kirklevington. Drew Pease's Plantation; very fast twenty-five minutes to ground. Went off to draw Staindale; capital gallop for thirty minutes to ground at Deighton. A screaming scent all day, and my diary says, 'A very good day's sport.'"

My Hunt Secretary was Mr. A. Park of Newbus Grange, who kept a watchful eye on the coverts, the finances, and other affairs of the Hunt, and I must not forget the names of one or two old Hurworth friends of those days who have since passed away.

There was Tom Wilkinson of Neasham Abbey, a keen sportsman who often acted as field-master when I was hunting the hounds. He kept a pack of otter-hounds, and was devoted to that pursuit; indeed it was from a chill which he caught on the river at his favourite summer sport that he died, after a short illness, in the prime of life many years ago. As Wordsworth puts it—" A man he was, of cheerful yesterdays and confident to-morrows," much beloved in his own country.

Then there was Lord Henry Vane-Tempest, who often turned up from Wynyard and elsewhere to have a day with us. He thought there was nothing like the Hurworth, and would travel any

LADY GRAHAM

distance to reach them. On his celebrated grey horse Cracker no one could beat and very few follow him; but probably that was the case with him on any horse and in any country.

It always delighted me to find him at the meet, as, if it was a likely hunting morning and everything promised well, he would invariably ride up to me, pointing his whip first at the Blankney bitches and then towards the sky, murmuring in confidential accents, " There's blood in the air to-day," evidently the happy omen being in his mind that we should certainly catch a fox before it was dark.

During his later years he hunted chiefly from Melton Mowbray, and it was there that he died very suddenly in January 1905. Kindly and courteous by nature, he was deeply and widely regretted by all who knew him.

At that time, when living at Norton Conyers, a long twenty-seven miles from the Hurworth Kennels, I found the pilgrimage to and fro on hunting days rather more than I could well manage, but no distance was too far and no weather too bad for Lady Graham, who was out almost every day.

There were no motors in those days, and the railway opportunities were often a most uncertain advantage at the end of a long run, when the afternoons were short of daylight; but there were other considerations also which induced me to resign.

My successor was Mr. William Forbes of Callendar, who had much previous experience as Master of the Kildare Hounds in Ireland. I sold my Blankney lot to Lord Chesham, who at that time had the Bicester, and it was with very great regret I said farewell to the Hurworth country on the 1st May 1888.

CHAPTER VIII

NORTON CONYERS

NORTON CONYERS is situated on the river Yore some four miles north of the city of Ripon; there is some difficulty in fixing the exact date when the quaint old house was built, but no doubt can exist that it was standing in the reign of Henry VII.

The ancient family of Norton were in possession from very early times until they became involved in the Rising of the North in 1569. A remarkable chapter of English history was that in which those who clung to the old faith staked their lives in its cause, many perishing; while others like the Earl of Westmorland, who left historic Raby behind him, and the venerable Richard Norton, fled to Flanders and were known in England no more.

The story of Norton was taken by Wordsworth as the theme of his " White Doe of Rylstone," in which he accepts the tale as told in the old ballad of the mission of Earl Percy's little foot-page to Master Norton, a summons which he could not resist :

> "'Come you hither, my nine good sonnes,
> Gallant men I trowe you be,
> How many of you, my children deare,
> Will stand by that good erle and me.'
>
> Eight of them did answer make,
> Eight of them spake hastilie,
> 'Oh father, till the day we dye,
> We'll stand by that good erle and thee.'"

And so went forth old Richard Norton with his banner bearing the cross and the five wounds of our Lord. His family were entirely ruined and his estates confiscated, though only one of his sons was executed, while he himself escaped to the Low Countries.

After the attainder of the Nortons, their estates were forfeited to the Crown, and subsequently Norton Conyers passed by a marriage with the Musgraves to the Grahams, descended through "John of the Bright Sword" from the Scottish Earls of Monteith and Strathearn. The first of the Grahams at Norton Conyers was the Royalist Sir Richard Graham "of the Netherby clan," who had married the daughter and heiress of Thomas Musgrave. He was Gentleman of the Horse to James I., was created a Baronet in 1629, and distinguished himself at

THE HALL AT NORTON CONYERS

FOX-HUNTING RECOLLECTIONS 127

Edgehill and Marston Moor, where he was desperately wounded and rode from the field of battle many miles to Norton, then through the Hall and up the stairway, where the print of the horse's hoof is still shown to this day.

The exterior of the Manor House has but little claim to architectural beauty, but it falls well into its woodland surroundings of sycamores and other trees of great size.

On the northern side is the historic bowling-green on which King Charles I. passed five consecutive days in his favourite amusement while waiting for supplies.

Within the old oak hall, covered with ancestral portraits, is the broad staircase of the legend, ascending by the big mullioned window with many coats-of-arms towards the panelled King's Room, which was occupied by more than one of the Royal Stuarts.

Many generations of Grahams had come and gone from the old house at Norton before the time of the last Sir Bellingham, born in 1789 and for seventy years a Baronet.

One point of special interest in connection with Norton Conyers is, that many consider it to be the original of " Thornfield Hall " in *Jane Eyre,* that most fascinating of all the Brontë works, though others lean to the belief that the place was intended for the "Rydings" near Birstall.

In that interesting book, the *Brontë Country*, Mr. Erskine Stuart expresses his conviction that Charlotte Brontë had Norton Conyers in her mind, and he gives many reasons for his opinion in the following words:—" There are also the rookery and the gardens; but this is not all, the interior of the hall oak, panelled and covered with portraits of men in armour, the brass handles and the double doors, the untenanted upper storey, the position of the housekeeper's room, and the broad oak staircase, all answer to the description in *Jane Eyre*."

Halfway between historic Ripon and the old Marmion Tower at Tanfield, in the picturesque valley of the Yore, in a country rich in natural beauty and full of history, there stands the old gabled house of Norton. The adjacent lands and woods, following the course of the river, are situated on the south side of what is known as the Bedale country.

The Bedale Hunt lies almost entirely in the North Riding; on the north it adjoins Lord Zetland's territory, on the east the Hurworth, and on the south the York and Ainsty.

The country originally formed part of the immense Raby Hunt so long hunted by the Earl of Darlington (afterwards Duke of Cleveland), but owing to failing health he gave up that portion which has since been called the Bedale Hunt, in 1832; and at that date Mr. Mark Milbank of Thorp Perrow became the Bedale Master, his reign extending to 1856. During the early part of his career Mr. Milbank hunted the hounds himself, and his two whippers-in were named Barwick and Mason. About twenty couples of his hounds came from Scotland, and the remainder consisted of drafts from other packs. Although coming from so many sources into a new country, his pack seems to have had fair success, as during their first season they hunted on seventy-three days and killed forty-six foxes. In their second season they hunted ninety-six days and killed seventy foxes.

Why is it, I wonder, that a new pack collected by drafts from many kennels, and all strange to one another, should at first almost invariably work well together and catch their foxes?

On this subject Beckford had something to say, for he tells us: "There is a pack now in my neighbourhood, of all sorts and sizes, which seldom miss a fox. When they run there is a long string of them, and every fault is hit off by an old southern hound. However, out of the last eighteen foxes they hunted they killed seventeen, and I have no doubt as they become more complete more foxes will escape from them. Packs which are composed of hounds of various kinds seldom run well together, nor do their tongues harmonise, yet they generally, I think, kill most foxes; but I must confess that, unless I like their style of killing them, whatever may be their success, I cannot be completely satisfied."

I can well remember old Squire Milbank: in fact he blooded me out on a pony with his hounds when about five years old, not many yards from the spot where the Bedale Hunt assemble in the present day whenever they meet at Norton Conyers once or twice in the course of every winter. His Mastership seems to have been successful, as the Hunt picture (of which the engraving is so well known) bears the following inscription:

"Presented to Mark Milbank, Esq., 17th December 1842, by members of the Bedale Hunt and other gentlemen, at the annual Hunt Dinner given by him as Master of the Bedale Hounds."

Portraits of the following gentlemen appear in the picture: Mr. Milbank and his hunt servants, Lord Zetland, Duke of Leeds, Duke of Cleveland, Sir Bellingham Graham, Colonel Pepper Arden, Mr. Sergeantson, Hon. Sackville Lane Fox, Hon.

John Dundas, M.P., Hon. Thomas Dundas, M.P., Capt. Van Straubenzee, Major Healey, Mr. Anthony Maynard, Mr. John Booth, Sir John Beresford, Sir Edward Dodsworth, Mr. John Bell of Thirsk, and others.

Then again in 1838 we find that a Bedale Hunt Song was composed in his honour by the Rev. John Monson, the Rector of Bedale, an excellent sportsman and very hard rider, of whom Lord Darlington in one of his diaries says: " I cannot omit to mention that the Rev. John Monson shone as conspicuously this day on his grey mare as in the pulpit, and was alone with the hounds over Ainderby Mires when they killed at last, near Thornhills willow bed."

There is an old Latin proverb which, when converted into English says: " If a man is not born a poet you cannot make him one," and I think that anyone will be inclined to agree with that maxim who reads the following ditty, which some fifty or sixty years ago was invariably sung year after year at every Bedale Hunt Club Dinner with acclamation :—

THE BEDALE HOUNDS IN 1838

"Here's to the old ones of fox-hunting fame,
    Cleveland, Ralph Lambton, and Harewood ;
Here's to the young ones that after them came,
    Who will not say that they are good ?

FOX-HUNTING RECOLLECTIONS

Here's to the Master[1] well skilled in the art
  To kill an old fox in all weathers;
Here's to the riders, all ready to start,
  Brilliant in boots and in leathers.

Here's to the hounds, all vigour and bone,
  In condition excelling all others;
Here's to old Barwick,[2] who stands quite alone
  In cheering them on through the covers.

Here's to the Sportsmen, I give you each name,
  Their feats and their fortunes in detail;
North Riding heroes, all eager for fame,
  To be reaped in the country of Bedale.

On Borderer mounted see Milbank ride,
  Three hundred won't buy such a horse, sir;
Limbs with no check to their freedom of stride,
  Wind without whistle or cough, sir.

'Tally Ho! Toot-a-toot! he is gone,' says the Squire;
  Let any one catch them who can, sir,
Who rides with my hounds a good horse will require,
  And himself he must be a good man, sir.

Here's to the Duke,[3] if he leads not still Leeds,
  To borrow a joke from His Grace, sir;
A nobleman true, both in word and in deeds,
  And the firmest support of the chase, sir.

Here's to the Graeme,[4] who does not disdain
  In a north-country province to ride, sir;
Forgetting that once, thro' the Leicestershire plain,
  Scarce a rival could live by his side, sir.

[1] Mr. Milbank of Thorp Perrow, died 1882.
[2] Mr. Milbank's first whip.
[3] The 6th Duke of Leeds.
[4] Sir Bellingham Graham.

FOX-HUNTING RECOLLECTIONS

Here's to the Colonel,[1] if warm be his name,
  Both that and his heart go together;
In pleasant discourse, whilst we ride down the lane,
  Let us be in no hurry to sever.

Here's to friend George, the beau of Camphill,
  A good one, if fast be the chase, sir,
To pass him, I tell you, requires as much skill
  As Fieschi, when he won the race, sir.

Here's to the Baron of Sawley, so sly,—
  Here's to his horse that is black, sir;
Forgetting that always a crow cannot fly,
  He fell o'er a fence on his back, sir.

Here's to Straubenzee, the dashing and bold,
  Taking all in his stroke like a man, sir;
And the pith of the story remains to be told—
  You can't shake him off from the 'Van,' sir.

Here's to the Major, the gallant and true,
  In riding to no one he'll yield, sir;
See, he brings by his side a young damsel in view,
  To beat half the men in the field, sir.

Here's to Dundases,[2] both Thomas and John,
  They come but to make us remember
How short is their stay—for to London they're gone
  Ere the end of the month of November.

Here's to the young ones, whose race scarce begun,
  Young Mark, and the ensign, his brother;
They show of a stock most goodly they come,
  As they tread in the steps of their father.[3]

[1] Colonel Pepper Arden.
[2] Sons of the 1st Earl of Zetland.
[3] Mr. Milbank's sons.

The gallant, the ardent, of promise so fair,
  The Beresford brothers they bring;
A word from my pen must give them their share
  Of the honours and glories I sing.

Many good ones remain—Hodgson, Crompton, and Tower,
  Fox, Ward, and the young one from Norton;
But to mention them all is not in my power,
  So, surely, it cannot be thought on.

And here's to the Squire of Thirsk, Jack Bell,[1]
  Who supports both the chase and the turf, sir;
He will not, unless he likes it, go well,
  Tho' the hounds may run ever so fast, sir.

Here's a bumper to Milbank, the source of our sport—
  A bumper to him and his hounds, sir;
Brim-full it shall be of the finest old Port,
  Where health and good humour abound, sir.

And may we all flourish till green our old age is,
  Such fun and such sport to pursue, sir;
And your 'lame' humble poet to be hanged now engages
  If his composition's not true, sir."

By the Rev. JOHN MONSON,
Rector of Bedale, 1838.

After Mark Milbank came the Hon. Ernest Duncombe (now Earl of Feversham) for eleven years; then Mr. John Booth of Killerby for another eleven years; but when he started the country does not seem to have been in a prosperous state, as during his first season his pack only killed eleven foxes and had fourteen blank

[1] Master of the Hambleton Hounds.

days. Later on matters improved and he showed some good sport, hunting them himself until he retired in the summer of 1878. After his time there were many Masters of the Bedale, including Major Dent, Mr. G. W. Elliot, M.P., Captain Wilson Todd, and the Duke of Leeds. To all of these Fred Holland was huntsman, a keen and cheerful man much liked by the farmers, who retired in 1902, after twenty years' service, with a testimonial of about £1000, and went to live at Masham, where he recently died.

The Duke of Leeds hunted the country regardless of expense for six seasons, from 1898 to 1904. I think the best day which I saw in his time was on the 24th January 1900, when he was hunting the hounds himself. They met at Norton Conyers and found a real good fox in Guy's Whin; ran by Nosterfield nearly to Low Park; then to the right, crossing the Bedale Road between Carthorpe and Burneston, up to Leeming Lane, where he was headed and turned short back, leaving Kirkington on his right, down to Sutton Howgrave across Parkfield Farm to the covert where he was found. Luckily they did not change there, and he went away over the South Park at Norton, where I saw him nearly done, but he managed to jump the high wall near our Ripon Lodge gates. Only about half the pack got over the wall, but they coursed him in view and caught him in the open at the end of the next field. It was a very good run, and I never saw anyone more delighted than the Duke was at the finish, when he and Mr. Amcotts Wilson started on their homeward journey of fifteen miles from Norton Conyers to Hornby Castle. It was a very old dog-fox, and he kindly had the head mounted and sent to our house, where it hangs to this day.

A few days later I had a tombstone placed on the spot to commemorate the event, with " Hic Jacet " and the date thereon. The Bedale second whipper-in at that time had rather a hump on his back, and went by the nickname of " Humpy." This hump almost seemed to act as an accumulator, for he had a singularly shrill hallo. The following season the hounds were trotting along to draw, and, as we passed this spot, I pointed with my whip towards the tombstone, and said to " Humpy," " You remember what happened there ? " He had not a retentive memory apparently, for he at once exclaimed, " Poor gentleman! was he killed on the spot ? "

On the Duke's retirement the Hunt, in appreciation of his services, presented him with a testimonial in the form of a silver fox, from a

FOX-HUNTING RECOLLECTIONS 137

model which had formerly been designed by Sir Edgar Boehm.

In 1904, Mr. Moubray started as the new Master, with Frank Freeman as his huntsman, and probably the present excellence of the pack is to some extent due to the way in which he handled them for two seasons. It was an unlucky day for the Master and the Hunt when Freeman forsook the Bedale for the white collar of the Pytchley.

Another northern Pack is Lord Zetland's, formerly the old Raby Hunt, which was hunted by Lord Darlington (afterwards 1st Duke of Cleveland), for at least fifty years. He began with a turn of the Badsworth country, where he was celebrated in song as follows:

"Then first in the burst, see dashing away,
 Taking all in his stroke on Ralpho the grey;
 With persuaders in flank, comes Darlington's peer,
 With his chin sticking out and his cap on one ear."

He then undertook the immense territory of both the Raby and the Bedale countries, until he gave up the latter in 1832, the former in 1839, and died in 1842. Throughout life he was also an immense pillar on the turf, and the pink-and-black stripes were victorious all over England.

When "Nimrod" visited Yorkshire in 1826, Lord Darlington was then in his 37th season and at that time it was asserted that, except upon occasions when duty called him to the House of Lords, he had only missed three days with his pack during that long period.

It was said that he never shirked any part of the hunting business by leaving it to others, but was content to go through the cub-hunting himself season after season.

In those days there was probably no other record in the history of sport which could compare with the description of that famous establishment at Raby, as during Lord Darlington's long reign the Hunt was maintained entirely by his own resources, and the scale upon which matters were conducted is perhaps shown by the fact that he paid £340 a year to his tenants north of the Tees for the rent of his own fox coverts.

However long the day's work, he never missed making notes of the sport in his Diary before that day was over, and this hunting chronicle he allowed to be published from year to year under the name of "The Operations of the Raby Pack."

After his death in 1842, at the age of seventy-six, he was succeeded by his son, who afterwards became known as Duke Henry. As the country had not been hunted for the previous three or four years, some of the fox coverts had got into bad

FOX-HUNTING RECOLLECTIONS 139

condition, and many of them had disappeared altogether, so Duke Henry established a pack of staghounds for some time; but after the coverts were restored and foxes had again became plentiful, he turned his staghounds into foxhounds, took possession of the old Raby country, and all went well for some years to come.

When this duke died in 1861 the same state of things appears to have occurred again, until 1866, when Mr. Cradock of Hartforth came to the rescue and started a pack, which he got together by drafts from various kennels. During his first season they hunted sixty-nine days, killed fourteen brace of foxes, and had five blank days. The second season of 1867-68 they hunted seventy-three days, killed ten brace, and had four blank days. Then in 1870, Thomas Bridger Champion was secured as huntsman, and matters continued to improve until Mr. Cradock's resignation in 1876, when the present Lord Zetland became M.F.H., and has since hunted the country.

Some years ago the members of his Hunt presented him with a picture, by Heywood Hardy; representing a meet of the hounds in front of Aske Hall. In addition to those of Lord Zetland, Champion, and other hunt servants, there were portraits of Sir William Eden of

Windlestone, Mr. Gilpin Brown of Sedbury, Mr. R. A. Morritt of Rokeby, Lord Londonderry, Lord Henry Vane-Tempest, Colonel Wilson of Cliffe, Captain Wilson Todd of Halnaby, Mr. Cradock of Hartforth, Mr. W. Scarth of Staindrop, Hon. Thomas Dundas, Lady Alice Dundas, Lady Hilda Dundas, Mr. Herbert Straker, Mr. J. Fife, Mr. W. Foster, and others; a pleasing picture, in which it is shown that now, as in the old days of Raby, the hunt still wear the black velvet collar and gold fox.

What real pleasure it was to hunt with Lord Zetland! Ever courteous and considerate to his field, he never deviated from the one object in his mind, and that was to show sport. To carry out that endeavour he was ably seconded by Champion, a brilliant man after a fox, a fine horseman, with a good voice, and keen to show a gallop at any hour of the morning or the evening; according to my views he was an ideal huntsman.

How many pleasant weeks year after year have I passed at Aske, that charming home of Lord and Lady Zetland, where hospitality is unbounded.

For the purpose of hunting in that country, I often stayed with Mr. Gilpin Brown at Sedbury, a sportsman of the old school who could go a long way back into history of the Raby Hunt.

At Rokeby also, that romantic spot beloved of Walter Scott:

> " 'Twas a fair scene. The sunbeam lay
> On battled tower and portal grey:
> And from the grassy slope he sees
> The Greta flow to meet the Tees;
> Where, issuing from her darksome bed,
> She caught the morning's eastern red,
> And through the softening vale below
> Roll'd her bright waves in rosy glow."

How often did I visit there in the time of Robert Ambrose Morritt, that humorous and vivacious Squire whose retentive memory and fund of anecdote rendered him a delightful companion and the best of company.

One word more about the old Raby Hounds. On reflection it seems a sad pity that an historic pack, hunted by such a celebrated sportsman as Lord Darlington for over fifty years, should have been dispersed to the winds by auction two or three years before he died in 1842. Where are the descendants nowadays of that once splendid pack?

One might almost as well ask what has become of Osbaldeston's noted blood, and where, indeed, are the descendants of his famous Furrier?

Sometimes we find in the present day that the celebrity of a distinguished M.F.H. hardly survives even his own lifetime.

A year or two ago I took up a weekly pictorial paper, with a picture intended to portray the meet of a pack of foxhounds somewhere in Leicestershire. In the foreground was represented an elderly gentleman on horseback in a hunting-coat and cap, and underneath were written these remarkable words: " The well-known octogenarian huntsman, ' Mr. Trilby,' was present on this occasion ! "

Throughout the sixties England was ringing with the heroic deeds of Mr. Tailby, and the hunting world were flocking into Market Harborough to follow Tailby and his brilliant pack over high Leicestershire. He did not even retire until 1878, and already his very name seems to be forgotten and distorted.

Trilby indeed, and such is fame!

Notwithstanding the attractions of the Bedale and Zetland Hunts, I could not be quite happy without some hounds of my own to hunt; therefore for several years I kept a pack of harriers at my own expense in the old kennels at Norton Conyers. We all know Jorrocks's opinion on the subject of harriers. Does he not say; " I never sees a chap a-trotting along the turnpike with a thick stick in his hand and a pipe in his mouth, but I says to myself, ' There goes a man well mounted for harriers.' I wouldn't be a Master of Muggers for no manner of money."

Such, however, were not my ideas on the subject, so I set to work to buy a pack from Scotland. Then various Masters of Hounds gave me a few small bitches which were hardly big enough for them to enter as foxhounds. Among others, Mr. Lycett Green kindly gave me five couples of beautiful animals from the York and Ainsty, some of them with Belvoir blood. I had to draft a good many of the Scotch lot before I could get them to the size and sort which I fancied, but at last I arrived at about fifteen couples, all bitches full of quality, and standing exactly 20 inches high.

The first man I had as kennel huntsman was Will Wootton, who came with the lot from Scotland, and I used to hunt them with him and a second horseman (in green coats and caps) to whip into me. After him a young fellow named Charles Greenhow took his place; and then in later years, Tom Champion from the Woodland Pytchley (a son of the huntsman whom I recently mentioned), a capital hound man and a nice fellow to go out with, who remained with me as long as I kept the harriers.

We had plenty of country, lots of grass for miles round Norton Conyers, and many good places to go to in the York and Ainsty country, notably the Copgrove Estate belonging to Admiral Sir Francis and Lady Bridgeman, where we had good sport, and were always welcome. Then Lord Harewood sometimes gave me a day or two about Goldsborough when he lived there; now and then, also, I had a day on the moors round about Harrogate, and Mr. Andrew Lawson of Aldborough, near Boroughbridge, often asked us over. Then in the Bedale country, Col. I'Anson of Howe, Mr. Nussey, M.P., of Rushwood, and other neighbours were all capital friends to the pack. Beckford once said, " It is a good diversion in a good country; you are always certain of sport; and if you really love to see your hounds hunt, the hare when properly hunted will show you more of it than any other animal."

I am quite sure that any boy who is destined to become a good sportsman should be entered early to harriers, not so much to teach him to ride, as to teach him not to ride in the wrong place and at the wrong time. With hare-hounds he will soon learn to pull up his pony at the least sign of a check, to sit still, to keep his eyes fixed on the pack, and to hold his tongue. It is only too evident in the present day that these simple lessons have not always been acquired in early

FOX-HUNTING RECOLLECTIONS 145

life by those who later on belong to the foxhunting community.

I derived immense enjoyment from the pursuit of the hare, though in my first season I found her a difficult animal to catch, and that as far as her own safety is concerned she has almost more cunning than the fox; but I soon became accustomed to their ways and to the proper system of hunting them. My own experience was not gained entirely from the habits of the Yorkshire hares, for that genial sportsman Lord Howth sent me over two or three dozen Irish hares, captured on his estate at Howth Castle. They were small in size, and in colour dark brown, some of them almost purple. I turned them down, and occasionally we found them again for the next year or two; they were a tough sort, and inclined to run more straight than the English hares, now and then giving quite a good point for harehunting.

My belief is that dwarf foxhounds can be taught to hunt a cunning hare as closely and as carefully as any old-fashioned southern harriers, and although my little pack went a good pace and were full of drive, they could also put their noses down with a moderate scent. As far as looks went they were quite up to Peterborough form, and just the sort I liked to walk about with on Sunday afternoons.

Over thirty years ago, when I was an M.F.H., I happened to be dining one evening at White's Club with the late Lord Suffolk, who at that time kept a pack of harriers at Charlton Park.

After dinner our conversation drifted into the discussion of hunting subjects, and as Mr. George Lane Fox was seated at an adjacent table not far off, Lord Suffolk fixed his glass in his eye (with him a sure sign of mischief) and boldly inquired from the celebrated Bramham Moor Master his opinion of hare-hunting. "I have always," he replied, "understood it to be a most scientific amusement."

It seems very doubtful if Peter Beckford really cared much for the pursuit of the hare; does he not tell us in his own words:

"I never was a hare-hunter. I followed this diversion more for air and exercise than amusement, and if I could have persuaded myself to ride on the turnpike road to the three-mile stone and back again, I should have thought I had no need of a pack of harriers."

Again, when contrasting the merits between the slow and the fast hounds for the purpose, he says:

VISCOUNT ANDOVER (AFTERWARDS EARL OF SUFFOLK) AND
SIR REGINALD GRAHAM, BART.
1867

"It was a difficult undertaking. I bred many years, and an infinity of hounds, before I could get what I wanted. I at last had the pleasure to see them very handsome, small, yet very bony; they ran remarkably well together, ran fast enough, had all the alacrity that you could desire, and would hunt the coldest scent. When they were thus perfect, I did as many others do, I parted with them."

This is exactly what I did myself in the spring of 1897, and I have never blown a horn again since that day. Perhaps I had blown my own trumpet quite enough already!

With the last century many sporting writers have come and gone, but amid all that hunting lore, what is there to compare with " My Winter Garden," that tale so descriptive of Charles Kingsley and his musings when a hunted fox crossed the path of his afternoon ride along the fir-clad heather lands which far and wide encircled his peaceful rectory at Eversley. Nothing in the English language can be more charming than the simple story he told us just fifty years ago.

Peter Beckford must have been about forty when he began his letters dated from " Bristol Hot Wells, 20th March 1779." He published them as a book in 1781, and called it *Thoughts on Hunting.* Since then there have been countless works on the same subject, but to this day Beckford still holds his own as our greatest authority, and some of his maxims might still be engraved in eternal brass.

What could be better than this ? " It is said, there is a pleasure in being mad, which only mad men know ; and it is the enthusiasm, I believe, of fox-hunting which is its best support ; strip it of that, and you then, I think, had better let it quite alone."

CHAPTER IX

SIR BELLINGHAM GRAHAM, BART.

As the hunting career of my father, Sir Bellingham Graham, took place long before my existence, I must of necessity have occasional recourse to the writers of those days for any record of what happened. It seems that he was an M.F.H. from 1815 to 1826, and between those dates he was Master of the Badsworth, Atherstone, Pytchley, Hambledon, Quorn, Albrighton, and Shropshire Hunts.

Born in 1789, he was just of age in 1810 when he established a pack of harriers at Norton Conyers, and had for his whipper-in a young man named Kit Atkinson, who had come from the Lord Strathmore of that day, and was destined in the future to become a celebrated hunt servant. These harriers were not confined to Yorkshire entirely, but were often taken into Sussex on a visit to the Sir Godfrey Webster of that time, who was then living at Battle Abbey. In Sussex they not only hunted hares, but on some occasions a stag was turned out for them.

This went on until the year 1815, when Sir

Bellingham became a Master of Fox Hounds by succeeding Mr. Musters in the Badsworth country. It is needless to say anything about that famous sportsman Mr. Musters, who was then acknowledged to be at the head of his profession, and if he had been as zealous in the details of the kennel as in those of the field, would have had a reputation second to none in England at that time ; as it was, Musters was a difficult Master to follow. Sir Bellingham appears to have hunted the Badsworth country for two years, and apparently with success. He hunted his hounds himself, with Jack Richards as first and Kit Atkinson as second whipper-in. Both these good servants remained until he took the Quorn six years later, when Jack returned to Badsworth as huntsman, and Kit was promoted to the same post in Worcestershire.

Kit's chief mission was to make young horses into hunters, in which duty he was very capable, being a good horseman, endowed with excellent hands, and weighing only nine stone. There was a good illustration of Kit's nerve later in the Atherstone country where he was riding a mare which had shown no signs of making a hunter throughout her six years, and had given him some very bad falls. Kit, however, would not give up hope, and declared that " she was sure to make a good one some day." The hounds got into Annesley deer park later on, when Kit came to the pales first and cleared them, getting well over before anyone else had a try.

It was in 1816 (during his Badsworth period) that Sir Bellingham won the St. Leger with a mare called the Duchess, by Cardinal York, and it was in 1817 that he left the Badsworth to commence his Mastership of the Atherstone country, which he held for three years.

The Atherstone Hunt included a large tract of country which had seen many changes up to 1815, when that noted sportsman "Squire" Osbaldeston came from Nottinghamshire and brought his own pack to the Atherstone for a couple of seasons.

Sir Bellingham hunted the Atherstone hounds himself, living most of the time at Lindley Hall, near the town of Atherstone. His establishment enabled him to hunt five days a week, and his management apparently gave satisfaction during the three seasons he remained there, as "Nimrod," in his *Hunting Reminiscences*, writes thus :

"It was a pleasure to any real sportsman to hunt with Sir Bellingham Graham, because he did the thing throughout in a thorough sportsmanlike style, as fox-hunting ought to be done ; from the moment he got upon his hunter until he killed or lost his fox he was intent and earnest in that pursuit, and the result of his sportsmanlike conduct was that no man kept his field in such good order.

"When Sir Bellingham Graham quitted the Atherstone country he left behind him a great regard for his good name and universal regret at his departure."

In the year 1820, fascinated by the idea of Northamptonshire, he left the Atherstone for the Pytchley, where he succeeded Lord Althorp and Sir Charles Knightley, but there he only remained for one season. Troubles of some kind seem to have arisen which rendered him unpopular in that country. The "Druid" records that "the foxes were destroyed, even the mail-coaches were hung with their dead carcases as a sort of defiance. Still, he fought on, and determined to have a grand field day. He turned down seven brace one night, but not a hound could speak to it in the morning, and he drew every covert blank again." The result was that at the end of the season he left the Pytchley to take over a very different style of country, namely, the Hambledon Hunt in Hampshire.

He undertook that country for three seasons from 1821, but as a matter of fact he was only there for a few months when the Quorn country was suddenly declared to be vacant.

Mr. Osbaldeston, who was the Master, addressed the members of the Quorn Hunt by a letter to the local papers, informing them of the fact that owing to a recent accident, when he broke his leg, he felt compelled to give up the country.

Sir Bellingham at once offered to take the Quorn, which he did through the same medium of the local paper, and the offer was immediately accepted. He purchased Osbaldeston's house, hounds, and horses, and arranged to leave a portion of his own pack with a whipper-in to fulfil his engagement with the Hambledon Hunt. How strange it sounds nowadays to hear of a Master retiring from a country by a letter to the county paper; but evidently there were no Hunt Committees in those days, and they seemed to have got on very well without them.

By taking the Quorn Sir Bellingham achieved the distinction, which he alone shared with Osbaldeston, of hunting that country as well as the famous Pytchley. They appear to have been on good terms together, as the Squire went off to Hampshire in his place and hunted the Hambledon country for one season.

The hunt servants to the Quorn at this time were Will Staples and Jack Wigglesworth; the hounds consisted of Sir Bellingham's original pack in addition to his purchase of all Osbaldeston's hounds, with the exception of twenty-five couples.

At this period the Quorn subscription amounted to between three and four thousand pounds, and Sir Francis Burdett, who was one of the principal subscribers, wrote: "Put me down for £300, and if that is not enough I am good for £200 more."

"Nimrod" tells us much about the good sport of that time, and that during one of the seasons the "old pack" killed every fox they found during the first six weeks. We are also told by the same writer that, as regards riding, Sir Bellingham had quite established his reputation as a leader among the best heavy-weights of that day. There was a celebrated run from Glen Gorse to Stanton Wood, for example, where he particularly distinguished himself on a horse called Cock Robin by taking the lead and keeping it until the finish, although two of the best light-weights in England, Colonel William Coke and Colonel George Anson, started within half a field of him, but never caught him until all was over.

It was about this time that his hunters became

SIR B. GRAHAM'S "TREACLE"
1823

so famous. The "Druid" tells us that Lord Plymouth, who could never be called a hard rider, gave Sir Bellingham a thousand guineas for Beeswax and Freemason, and that he seldom sold the horses of his own riding for less than four hundred guineas each : Parchment, The Baron, and Treacle all went to Mr. Maxse at this figure; so did that handsome grey horse Hesperus, a wonderful animal over deep country, who went into Mr. Foljambe's hands at the same price; but Will Butler, to whom he was assigned, had to do all his cub-hunting on him that season before he could get him quiet enough to suit them there.

There seems no record of what became of those celebrated hunters Paul, Jerry, and Norton Conyers, a chestnut horse who could manage twenty stone and was a splendid gate-jumper.

From the pictures of these horses which are in my possession it seems as if most of them could have carried at least eighteen stone, not far off the weight which their owner must have required from them.

In the portrait of Treacle there is a likeness of John Pulfrey, the old stud groom, who after many years of long and faithful service was settled in one of the Norton farms, where he died on the 1st July 1864, aged eighty-three.

One year during the summer months a country-looking fellow called upon the Baronet at his London house and asked him if he would sell two of his horses. He said he would, that they were down at Norton Conyers, and that the price was one thousand guineas. The man paid the sum in bank notes then and there, and the horses were never heard of afterwards.

Some time later the same man called again and asked the price of Beeswax. He was told five hundred guineas. "As I've been a good customer, I hope you'll make it pounds," said the man. "I'll see you damned first," was the prompt reply.

As a huntsman the critics seem to have found little fault with Sir Bellingham, except that he was perhaps too quiet in drawing, and was therefore at some times apt to draw over his fox; but his horses and horsemanship were so good that he was never long without having an eye on his hounds, and being able to assist them when in a difficulty.

It would appear that his custom was to divide his hounds for hunting days into an old pack and a young pack, and it is possible that this system may have had some advantages as regards uniform pace, but it is doubtful if the practice would find much favour with huntsmen of the present day.

"Nimrod" describes the circumstances of a very severe fall he had with the Quorn.

" He was killing his fox at the end of a sharp thing when an ox fence presented itself. Three first-rate performers were going in the same line, but they would not have it. Sir Bellingham never turned his horse, and cleared all but the rail on the opposite side, which probably his weight would have broken; but unfortunately his horse alighted on one of the posts, and turned over on the rider's chest. Strange as it may appear, Sir Bellingham remounted his horse and rode on; but he had not proceeded many yards when he was observed by Sir Harry Goodricke to be in the act of falling to the ground, but which he was fortunate enough to prevent. From that period, about twelve at noon till nine the next night, Sir Bellingham never knew what had happened to him: and as he lay under the haystack—whither his friends removed him at the time of the accident—every moment was expected to be his last. The pith of the story, however, is yet to come. He was bled three times the first day, and confined to his bed five. On the seventh, to the utter surprise, and indeed annoyance, of his friends, he was seen in his carriage at Scraptoft, merely, as he said, ' to see his hounds throw off.' The carriage not being able to get up to the spinney, Sir Bellingham mounted a quiet old horse, placed there, no doubt, for the purpose, muffled up in a great coat and a shawl, and looked on. The fox was found, but took a short ring and returned, when the hounds came to a check close to where he was sitting upon his horse. Will Beck, the huntsman *pro tem.*, not being up with his hounds, the Baronet cast them and recovered his fox. In three fields they checked again, and Beck made a slow but by no means brilliant cast. Sir Bellingham saw all this from the hill, and, no longer a looker-on, he cantered down to his pack and hit off his fox again. Things still went on but awkwardly. Another error was observed, when Sir Bellingham, annoyed that a large field should be disappointed of their sport when there was a possibility of having it, took a horn from the whipper-in (for he could not speak to them) and got to work again. The hounds mended their pace; down went the shawl in the middle of a field. They improved upon it; down went the great-coat in another field; then he stuck to his hounds in a long hunting run of an hour and a half over a strongly fenced country, and had got his fox dead beat before him, when he was halloed away by one of his own men to a fresh fox under the Newton Hills.

"Now what is to be done? The excitement that had carried him thus far was all gone, and it was all but whoo-hoop. With every appearance of exhaustion, and a face as pale as if he were dead, he sat himself down on a bank and faintly exclaimed, 'How am I to get home, Heaven only knows.'"

SIR BELLINGHAM GRAHAM, BART., ON THE "BARON"
1823

It was during this Mastership of the Quorn Hunt that Ferneley, the well-known artist, painted at Melton Mowbray, in 1822, the celebrated Quorn picture which included the following portraits :

Hon. Captain Berkeley, R.N., Hon. George Anson, Val· Maher, Sir Bellingham Graham (on The Baron), Lord Brudenell, Lord Rancliffe, Mr. Whyte - Melville, Mr. Greene of Rolleston, Lord Elcho, Mr. Maxse (on Cognac), Mr. George Wombwell, Marquis of Graham, John Moore, Colonel Coke (on Advance), Sir James Musgrave, Lord Molyneux, Lord Darlington, John Bushe, Jack White, Ferneley (the artist).

This picture still hangs in the hall at Norton Conyers, and is said to have cost £2000, a price which alarmed the Meltonians of those days, with the result that it was eventually raffled for at £100 a-piece. It had been arranged that the winner should be declared by throwing dice, and most of the competitors were present. Sir Bellingham was not there, but was represented by Mr. Maxse, who, after throwing six and five for himself, had one more throw for his absent friend, which turned out to be double sixes, and this won the prize, appropriately enough, for the Master of the Quorn.

In 1823, Osbaldeston returned to the Quorn,

repurchasing twenty-five couples of his old pack for £1000, and continued to hunt the country up to 1827, when he took the Pytchley. His favourite hounds were Furrier, Flourisher, Vaulter, Rasselas, Valentine, Hermit, and Rocket. At one time there were twenty-four and a half couples by Furrier, a black-and-white dog, who was bred at Belvoir in 1821 by Saladin from Fallacy. The Squire sometimes made the whole of his pack for the day's hunting of hounds by that noted sire. In 1834 he retired for ever as M.F.H., and transferred his hounds privately and conditionally to Mr. Harvey Combe, who took them to the Old Berkeley Kennels at Rickmansworth. In 1840, still described as "Mr. Osbaldeston's hounds," they were sold in lots at Tattersall's and realised £6400, but most of them went back to Mr. Harvey Combe, and Lord Cardigan bought ten couples to remain in the Pytchley country.

How interesting it would be nowadays to know where any of that once famous foxhound blood is to be found!

Upon the retirement of the famous John Mytton from the Mastership of the Albrighton Hunt in 1822, no one could be found to take over the whole of his country, and the sportsmen of the district had to rely upon Mr. William Hay, who hunted the Staffordshire side only from kennels at Market Drayton, during the season of 1822. At a meeting presided over by Mr. F. Holyoake, held on the 26th February 1823 at the Lion Inn, Wolverhampton, a committee was appointed to raise a subscription of £1000, which the meeting considered would be sufficient for hunting the country two days a week from kennels in any central position, and to discover "a proper person to take the management." Only a few days later the committee found such a person in Sir Bellingham Graham, who in a memorandum dated 1st March, agreed to hunt the country three days a week for the subscription named.

He accordingly rented Compton House, near Kinver, where kennels were built; he used also Mr. Mytton's old kennels at Ivetsey Bank for temporary accommodation when the meets were on that side. He was not, however, satisfied with the sport he showed during the winter 1823-4, for on 5th February it was intimated at a meeting at the Lion Hotel that, having given the country a fair trial, Sir Bellingham had come to the opinion that it would not afford foxes for three days a week with good sport, and that he proposed accepting an invitation he had received from Shrewsbury with the promise of a subscription, to hunt part of the Shropshire country. He undertook, therefore, to hunt the Albrighton and the Shropshire each four days in alternate fortnights, and hoped this plan would meet the continued support of the Albrighton subscribers.

The arrangement was not altogether successful, and at the end of the season 1824-5, Sir Bellingham resigned the Albrighton, and restricted himself entirely to Shropshire.

He had in 1823 taken a house situated upon the Whitchurch Road, within a mile and a half of Shrewsbury, the property of Mr. Loxdale the Town Clerk, and here in that year the gentlemen of the Shrewsbury side of the county had subscribed to build kennels capable of holding a hundred couple of hounds, with stabling for twenty-six hunters and six loose boxes. There was also a temporary kennel at Lee Bridge for the meets on the Prees side, which contained some of the best coverts.

The country itself was well off for foxes, and would stand four days a week. On the whole, too, it held a fair scent, but it was deficient in gorse coverts generally, and in those days a great part of it was wet and boggy and difficult to stop. As a country to ride over, Shropshire was easy, so far as fencing was concerned; there was nothing to stop a hard rider fairly well mounted, seldom any necessity to take timber, and the common Shropshire fence was a small hedge on a low bank with only a single ditch. These fences, however, came quickly, had to be taken slowly, and were very apt to stop horses in their pace, especially as the going was almost always in deep ground. In one part of the country, also, the low-lying meadows abound with black boggy drains, which will not allow a horse approaching near enough to be certain of clearing them; and it may be said of the Shropshire country, as a whole, that a horse which can go well there can go well anywhere.

In Shropshire, accordingly, Sir Bellingham maintained a hunting establishment little inferior to that he had considered necessary for Leicestershire. His kennels contained seventy couples of working hounds, and his stables twenty-six weight-carrying hunters. Large hounds did not suit the small enclosures of Shropshire, and there were some in the dog pack bigger than were desirable.

Vulcan was a favourite hound, but determined and savage if put out. On one occasion when running hare, Joe Maiden, then second whip, caught him a " broadsider " for it ; Vulcan jumped at him and bit him right through boot and stirrup-leather. Virgin, by Cheshire Valiant, from Fancy by Lord Lonsdale's Palafox, was another favourite, a bitch which remained good for eight seasons. Workman, by Wildboy, by Osbaldeston's Wonder from Remnant, was a hound which could run for ever; Patience, too, by Abelard out of Purity, and full of the old Pytchley blood; Brimstone, by Marmion from Jezebel; Famous, by Lord Lonsdale's Reveller from Sir B's Factious; Juliet, Jollity, and Jealous by Osbaldeston's Piper from Lord Lonsdale's Joyful; Purity and Parasol, from Mr. Warde's pack, were all famous hounds.

"Nimrod" has an interesting account of the kennel management of the Shropshire hounds under Will Staples:

" He throws open the door of the feeding-house and stands at a certain distance from it himself. He draws a certain number of hounds, calling them by their names. He then turns his back upon the open doorway and walks up and down the troughs, ordering back such hounds as he thinks have fed sufficiently. During this time not a hound stirs beyond the sill of the open door. One remarkable instance of discipline presented itself on this day. Vulcan, the crowning ornament of the dog pack, was standing near the door waiting for his name to be called. I happened to mention it, though rather in an undertone, when in he came and licked Sir Bellingham's hand: but though his head was close to the trough and the grateful viands smoking under his nose, he never attempted to eat; but on his master saying to him, ' Go back, Vulcan, you have no business here,' he immediately retreated and mixed with the hungry crowd."

"Nimrod" has also left a full record of the hunting of 1825-6, and of the characters of some of the more famous of the hard-riding gentlemen of those days. Mr. Lyster of Rowton, Lloyd of Aston, Councillor Slaney of Shrewsbury, Wynne the Shrewsbury surgeon, and, of course, the eccentric Jack Mytton. One may read in his pages of famous runs from the favourite meets. Arcall Mill, with its gorse covert, a rarity in Shropshire; of a run of forty-five minutes from Twemlows, the crack covert of the hunt, a run that was ended for all but the hounds by the Severn, which the bitch pack swam, and killed their fox by themselves in gallant style. "Nimrod" tells us, too, of a day at Acton Burnall, where he saw three gentlemen riding at gates all tumbling over their horses' heads without their horses falling, Jack Mytton, Mr. Rock, and Mr. Byrne from Ireland, this last sportsman going to a brook and wetting the knees of his breeches to enable him to stick to the saddle; of a splendid hour and forty minutes, too, from Babbins Wood, ending with a kill between Chirk Castle and Llangollen. One reads also of manners and customs long since discarded; how sober sportsmen had a poor chance against some of the others who were " a little primed," and how midday drinking was held to improve riding across country. " Why don't you tackle that Welsh Squire," asked Lord Forester of a friend who was much badgered by a sportsman from Wales. " Why, if I could be sure he would come out sober, I would take his bet to-morrow, but the infernal fellow will come out half-drunk and then he beats me," was the answer.

"The Druid," too, has a note on some of the traditions of the Shropshire Hunt at this period. "The Atcham Bridge Meet has never looked its best since the three (Will Staples, Jack Wigglesworth, and Tom Flint) were wont to wait in the meadow for Sir Bellingham. We know no spot so rich in hunting history, even if Jack Mytton had not jumped those rails with his arm in a sling."

I am grateful to various writers of former times from whom I have obtained information, but it is to " Æsop " (the Hampshire historian) I am indebted for a very characteristic anecdote:

"On taking his hounds into Hampshire to hunt the Hambledon country, Sir Bellingham inquired from the Hunt Secretary what amount of subscription would be forthcoming. 'About £700,' was the reply, upon which he contemptuously remarked, 'Barely enough to keep me in spur leathers and blacking.'"

It is quite possible that economy was not the strongest point in his character.

CHAPTER X

ATHERSTONE, 1817-1820

SOME extracts from a Diary of the Atherstone, Pytchley, and Quorn, kept between the years 1817 and 1823, may even at this distance of time be considered interesting, as they are taken from the handwriting of Sir Bellingham Graham, who hunted those celebrated countries.

In the autumn of 1817, his first season with the Atherstone, cub-hunting did not start till 30th September. Owing to absence of rain the ground was very hard, but in spite of the heat " the hounds behaved exceeding well."

Hounds hunted sixteen days up to 1st November, and killed nine foxes, of which there appeared to be a plentiful supply. The Diary mentions that one day thirty-three couples of hounds were out.

" October 8th. Hopwas Hays. — Thirty couples; found instantly, and went away down to Hints; turned to the right for Swinfen, through Swinfen Pool Tail, and killed in Mrs. Dyott's Plantation an old dog-fox—fifty-five minutes: very quick. Found again in Hopwas, and ran two foxes to ground in about an hour. Tried a small gorse of Mr. Floyer's; found, and ran down to Hints, where we ran from wood to wood, but so many foxes, and the hounds rather beat with their work in the morning, we could not kill one. Rode Squire and Richmond; Jack Richards, Milton; Kit Atkinson, Selim."

On October 15th, hounds did not leave off till after dark, a long day's cub-hunting, killed one early, but owing to changing could not get hold of a second.

The last half of the month was very windy, and on several occasions he went home early, " as hounds could not hear one another."

" October 27th. Hartshill Hays.—Twenty-three couples; found directly; drove him very quick through Bentley Park, and ran him to ground in a small covert of Mr. Dugdale's. Tried Arley Wood, where we found a brace of foxes; came away with one, past Close Wood, and down to Kinsbury Wood, at a terrible quick pace for fifty minutes, when a violent storm of wind and rain came on which entirely washed away every particle of scent; but for that he was dying fast. Rode Barber; Kit, Rat Tail; and Jack, Francis."

Even in those days a crowd was not unknown, as he says on 3rd November: " The greatest mob of horse and foot people I ever saw"; and on 1st December: " Such a concourse of Birmingham people were never seen."

"November 15th.—Nineteen couples at Odstone; found a brace of foxes in the gorse, one of which we ran direct through Nailstone Whigs, and over the open for forty minutes at the best pace on to the Forest; we then changed our fox, and after a great deal of severe running he went into a drain under the road by Bradgate Park wall, making on the whole two hours and twenty-five minutes, the first hour and five minutes without a check; opened the drain and got him out, an old dog-fox. My horse Exeter died the same evening. Rode Exeter and Houghton; Jack, Peter; Kit, Chicken.

"November 17th. Catton.—Twenty couples; found two or three foxes immediately, one of which we got well away with and ran a ring by Walton and back, when he threw himself into the earth, which had been opened in our absence, about ten yards before the leading hounds; a most terrible burst for thirty minutes, so quick that no horse could live with them. Found a disturbed fox in Seal Wood, which got away twenty minutes before us, and ran him with a stale scent down to Barton; Jack's horse so lame we were forced to leave him at Drakelow. Rode Derby and Richmond; Jack, Doctor; Kit, Chestnut Horse.

"December 2nd. Burbage.—Twenty couples; tried all the Tooley and Normanton Coverts, but did not find. Jack coming with my second horse, viewed a fox go into a small spinney near Kirkby, when we laid the hounds on, and ran a most terrible pace for fifty minutes through Kirkby Wood and pointing for Lindley, when the hounds ran from scent into view and killed close to Stoke Golding, an old bitch-fox; many Melton men out. Rode Houghton and Titus; Jack, Rocket; Kit, Selim.

"December 17th. Shuttington Bridge.—Twenty-three couples; tried Amington Decoy and the Frith blank; found in Hopwas; rattled him once or twice round the covert; went away, and ran him a desperate pace up to Money Moor Plantation, where he just beat the hounds to ground. Found a brace in the Brockhurst, one of which we ran round by Canwell, and he laid down in a pit in a wheat field, jumped up in view, and we ran into him nicely, close to the garden wall at Middleton; an hour and five minutes: a bitch-fox. Rode Houghton and Whittington; Jack, Rocket; Kit, Selim.

"December 19th. Biddlesfield.—Twenty-one couples; drew the wood and Aston Furze; found in Manley gorse, and chopped a bitch-fox. Another broke away at the same time, which we ran through Money Moor, Weeford Park, past Canwell, and over the enclosures to Drayton, where we ran from scent into view, and killed in the middle of Drayton Park. Striver and Traveller the two leading hounds; an old dog-fox. A pretty run of fifty-eight minutes. It came on to rain very hard, but the gentlemen wished us to try on, and found close to Middleton, but it poured so with rain we could do nothing. Rode

Derby and Crown Prince; Jack, Chestnut Horse; Kit, Charlotte.

"December 20th. Twycross.—Twenty-two couples; found at Gopsall; ran through Coton Gorse and down to Coton Village, where we lost him very unaccountably; I think he got into a drain. Drew Coton Gorse; found a brace; ran one very fast past Sibson over the brook in the bottom, past Shenton to Sutton Ambion, where Kit viewed him; lay down two or three times while we changed upon a fresh fox; stopped the hounds, and ran the hunted fox on to Bosworth, where the scent quite died away, owing, I think, to a violent hailstorm which came on very fast, and we gave him up—an exceeding good run of one hour and twenty minutes. Rode Titus and Contract; Jack, Peter; Kit, Chicken.

"January 13th, 1818. Arbury.—Eighteen couples; found directly in the Lodge covert; went away with him at the best pace, pointing for Nuneaton; he then turned and came a wide ring, pointing for Cowlees Wood, without a check; we there rather slackened our pace, and came by degrees to slow hunting; however, we got up to him at Ansley, and ran him sharp into Bentley Park, where, unfortunately, we had several on foot, and the wind so high we could not keep the hounds together; we therefore took them home; it was thirty-five minutes to Cowlees Wood, and one hour and twenty-five in all, a very good run. Rode Soldier and Cottager; Jack, Peter; Kit, Charlotte."

The next day his horse fell on his back into a drain, and had to be drawn out with horses; the hounds meanwhile ran fast from the Garden spinney near Bassets Pole, past Drayton and Middleton to ground at Hopwas.

A day or two later there is an insight into the trials of the huntsman even of that period: " A most infernal scent, and some of the Derbyshire sportsmen chose to hallo the hounds so much that they would not settle." On another occasion he says he was " glad to give up for the day, owing to a terrific confusion of scents (hounds were running two foxes) and a most ungovernable field, which brought us to repeated checks."

" January 20th. Burbage.—Eighteen couples; tried all the coverts blank; found in Kirkby Great Wood; ran very quick up to Newbold Village, the hounds pressing him hard; he then turned and we ran him back to Kirkby very much blown, and killed him; an old dog-fox. The first twenty minutes very good; in all, forty-five minutes. Tried the two gorses upon Newbold Heath; blank. Rode Houghton and Contract; Jack, Barley; Kit, Charlotte."

On January 27th they found at Amington Decoy, and ran fast to Statfold; the fox jumped the big garden wall, and went on to Thorpe, eventually being caught in the shrubberies; an old dog-fox.

"January 29th. Bassets Pole.—Nineteen couples; found in Trickley Coppice; ran very fast past Canwell, through the Hints Coverts, and caught view of him going out of Mill Ditch; he then turned back from distress, came through the Hints Coverts again, and finally killed him in a pig-sty after a very nice run of fifty-four minutes; a dog-fox. Rode Lupus upon trial. Went to Hopwas; found two or three foxes, but the day altered for the worse, and after persevering there two hours, went home. Rode Lupus and Titus; Jack, Derby; Kit, Charlotte.

"January 31st. Drakelow.—Eighteen couples; the ground covered with snow, and tremendous hailstorms every ten minutes. Some people had viewed a travelling fox as they came, and hoping he might stop we picked a scent nearly to Greasley Wood, but could not come up to him. Found at Seal Wood, and ran a tremendous pace for thirty minutes towards Clifton, and were on excellent terms, when, unfortunately, one of the cursed hailstorms came on, and every particle of scent disappeared. Rode Soldier and Squire; Jack, Midnight; Kit, Chicken.

"February 2nd. Chemsley.—Eighteen couples; the day was so frosty, we stopped with the hounds at Shustoke and drew the Shawberry Wood at one o'clock; found instantly. Ran him through Packington Park, where he bore to the left, and drove him across the country through Meriden Tan Yard, and on to Millison Wood, where we were just running into him when a fresh fox jumped up; came back through Meriden Shafts, and down to the woods where we first found, and had several foxes on foot directly, and at last with great difficulty contrived to stop the hounds, as our horses were all tired and it was nearly dark; an excellent scent, and ran three hours without a check. Rode Cottager; Jack, Doctor; Kit, Pomfret."

Just when they were having this excellent sport, a sharp frost came and stopped hunting till the 13th. On this day they were advertised to meet at Higham; it was barely fit to hunt, but being a "club day," he threw off at Weddington Wood. "Nobody out except Chetwode and Lloyd"; found, and ran past Stoke Gorse by Sutton Ambion to Bosworth, where hounds were stopped on account of the ground. Mention is made that Modesty got under the ice in crossing the canal and was drowned.

"February 17th. Twycross. — Eighteen couples; drew both the coverts at Coton and Gopsall blank; trotted away to Odstone, where we found in the Gorse; ran him very sharp by Nailstone Village through Nailstone Whigs, and straight up for Barden Hill, over the hill and on to Copt Oak Wood, where we got upon a brace of fresh foxes, and kept changing so often in the forest that at the last we stopped the hounds. Our first fox had lost half his brush. The thirty minutes up to Barden Hill was very good. Rode Houghton and Whittington; Jack, Peter; Kit, Charlotte.

"February 24th. Fisher's Mill.—Eighteen couples; found our old fox in the Middleton Garden Spinney; ran him very fast up to North Wood, through it and out three miles farther up the country; he then turned and came back at a racing pace through all those fine meadows in front of Kingsbury, crossed the river opposite Cliff close to where the ladies were in the boat, recrossed again below Fisher's Mill, and ran him to ground in a rabbit-hole inside the hedge of Trickley Coppice; dug and killed a dog-fox: an exceeding good run of one hour and twenty-five minutes. Rode Houghton and Lupus; Jack, Peter; Kit, Charlotte."

It seems as if he always liked to dig when he ran a fox to ground, and evidently thought more of his hounds than of his field, as on 5th March a fox having gone to ground just in front of the pack after a good run of nearly three hours, he dug for three hours more and then failed to get his fox.

His own, and also his hunt servants' horses, seem to have come out frequently, in spite of the open weather and hard work. Four of his own carried him on nearly twenty days each during the season. He mentions, however, that Jack— his first whip—had a heavy fall on 11th March at the end of a long day, and his horse had to be then and there destroyed.

A curious incident occurred a few days later. After a blank morning at Chillington and Boscobel, they found at the Lizard, and after running fast for fifty minutes were just catching their fox when he was coursed and killed by two butcher's dogs.

I have heard many different theories propounded as to scent or the want of it. A new idea appears in the account of 26th March: There having been a heavy fall of snow in the morning, " such immense flakes of snow kept falling from the trees that there was no scent at all in covert."

A day or two after, they had a capital gallop from a covert of Lord Anson's near Black Slough. Went away very fast through Fisherwick and on to Hopwas; up to there forty minutes without a check. " Hounds got a view of the fox going through the low part of the wood, but he went to ground just in front of them in one of the earths that had been drawn after stopping."

"April 13th. Hopwas.—Twenty-four couples; found a brace of foxes, one of which we ran to ground in the covert, the other went away. Drew Fisherwick; ran the best pace to Black Slough, thirty-three minutes: there came to a check owing to the fox being headed;

went on with him past General Dyotts, and to Long Green, where he was much beat and hung about the village. He, however, finally beat us near Lichfield, after an hour and three-quarters. The hounds behaved well all day. Rode Cottager and Richmond; Sir James Musgrave, Lupus; Mr. Hodgson, Soldier; Jack, Derby; Kit, Chicken."

The last day of the season was on 17th April, and unfortunately, blank, owing, he says, " and hopes," to the earths having only been put to in the morning; this, and the fact that some hounds got caught in traps, proved an unlucky finish.

Including cub-hunting, hounds hunted ninety-two days, of which three were blank, and killed forty-one foxes. The Diary says: "Capital scenting all November, and till Christmas, generally speaking, very good sport; after that weather was cold and stormy, with a good deal of frost, but little snow to lay."

Sir Bellingham had evidently greatly increased his kennel before starting on his second Atherstone season, as there is frequent mention of over forty couples being out, and one day the number actually reached fifty-one couples.

In the Diary there is a hound list giving names of old hounds in the kennels at the end of the last season; total, thirty-nine couples.

Not content with these and his young entry, he

bought, early in September, Mr. Newnham's pack from Worcestershire; of these when he first took them out hunting, he says: "Having been fed up for sale and uncommonly fat, they were by no means fit." All through the following season he used to divide the hounds into young and old packs, with an occasional mixed pack.

Cub-hunting started on 24th August 1818, when he says: "Having had no rain for some months the ground was in a worse state than in the hardest frost." However, they hunted, and eventually marked to ground; after digging for half an hour "it proved to be an old sow-badger." Some rain fell, and then they had capital sport with plenty of blood, so much so that, to quote the Diary on 26th September:

"Part of the hounds were running another cub hard, and it was so much blown that I was fearful they would kill it. However, we contrived to get them stopped.

"October 10th, 1818. Kirkby.—Twenty-eight couples; young pack. Found in the Willow bed; ran him past the house and over the open very fast for half an hour, when he went into a drain close to Desford; bolted him, and ran him a terrible pace for a quarter of an hour, when he went into another drain at the edge of Firley Brake; bolted and killed, a cub dog-fox. While the hounds were worrying him two more foxes came out of the same drain. Out of the first drain another fox bolted, and Jack got a third. Turned down the fox we had got, in front of Kirkby House, which we ran to ground in Fulshaw's earth; it had been scratched open by some other foxes. A good scent and a very nice day's sport. Rode Squire and Resin; Jack, Bluebeard; Kit, Galen.

"October 20th. Ridge Heath.—Twenty-two couples; old pack. Drew the Heath, and on it killed a bitch-fox with her leg in a trap. Found in a little covert close to Mr. Boycott's; ran him very fast over the Heath and some way towards Apley; he then turned, came back to Chesterton Rocks; from thence we viewed him away, and he went into a drain in the middle of a grass field; bolted and killed an old dog-fox; one hour and five minutes. Found three foxes in Snowden Pool. I was on the wrong side of the covert, and stopped five couples of hounds running one of the foxes. The body went by Molyneux's Gorse, past Badger, and nearly up to Apley; he then turned, and in coming back I met them, and we ran him to ground in the banks by Wrighton; one hour and three-quarters—in all a good day's sport. Rode Cottager; Jack, Sophy; Kit, Pomfret."

On October 24th, the Diary says: "Ran him very quick for two miles towards Shifnal, but the gentlemen chose to override the hounds so shamefully that they were soon brought to an irrecoverable check."

"October 29th. Apley.—Twenty-one couples; O. P. Found in the Long Coppice and ran very hard for some time. We then changed upon another fox, and, after running in the covert an hour and twenty minutes, killed a dog-fox. Drew the Ram Leys; found three foxes; went away very quick over the Canal, round by Mr. Botfields, over the Canal again, past the Collieries, through Wards Rough, and on to Sheriff Hales; he skirted the coverts and went on to Woodcot, where he had laid down in a wheat field; he then came back a wide ring, at the best pace, to the Sheriff Hales Woods, and we ran into her at the edge of the Abbey Wood: an old bitch-fox; two hours and sixteen minutes; a very excellent day's sport. Rode Beeswax, who went capitally; Jack, Francis; Kit, Warrior."

Cub-hunting thirty-three days, and killed twenty-eight foxes.

The Diary remarks: "September—first half very dry, afterwards wet and good scenting; October, a good scent in general." He appears to have had capital sport.

"November 4th. Whetstone. — Nineteen couples; O. P. Chopped a fox in the gorse; another fox went away instantly; the people pressed the hounds terribly, but we ran him pretty well for an hour and five minutes to Burbage, where we quite lost him. Went on to the wood, where we instantly hit upon him, and after running ten minutes in covert, killed the fox. Found in the wood and went away to Newnham for fifty-five minutes; the most beautiful thing possible, when just as we were killing him a fresh fox jumped up in the plantations; of course I stopped the hounds; a very excellent day's sport. Rode Titus and Squire; Jack, Bluebeard; Kit, Pomfret."

A good gallop took place on 10th November. Meeting at Twycross; found in Nailstone Whigs and went away up to the Forest, leaving Barden Hill on the left; straight over it, and down to Loughborough Oatwoods; there hounds were halloed on to a fresh fox and stopped; one hour and ten minutes.

"November 12th. Canwell. — Twenty-five couples; Y. P. Found in Weeford Park; ran him a little about the house and then took him off with a moderate scent towards Sutton Park, where he beat us. Found again in Manley Gorse, where we killed in covert a dog-fox. Drew Mill Ditch and the Brockhurst blank. Found again in Weeford Park at half-past three; ran him nearly to Manley Gorse, through Mill Ditch, the Brockhurst, back by Canwell, and into a rabbit earth in Weeford Park; dug and killed a dog-fox. A very nice run of one hour. Rode Houghton and Resin; Jack, Cumberland; Kit, Selim.

"November 21st. Merevale.—Twenty-three couples; Y.P. Found in Bentley Park, and ran very quick over to Oldbury; brought him back to the park, where we had three or four foxes on foot and the hounds all divided; got them together and recovered one of the foxes, who went away at the best pace for forty minutes, and we killed in a farmyard between Kingsbury and Coventry. Rode Cottager and Skylark; Jack, Leicester; Kit, Cumberland.

"November 27th. Newbold Gate.—Twenty couples; O. P. Found in the small gorse; ran him for fifteen minutes at the most bursting pace possible, and killed him, a young dog-fox. Found directly in the large gorse; ran him round by Ratby Burrows, nearly to Mackfield, back by the gorse, where he nearly beat us by slipping short back; but a farmer came and told me he had just seen him go into a drain in a grass field. Opened it, and got it out—an old bitch-fox; a good run, though a ring, for two hours. Rode Houghton and Squire; Jack, Bluebeard; Kit, Pomfret."

Evidently he was on very good terms with Osbaldeston, and this is shown by a note in the Diary : " Hunted him nicely down to Braunston, where I stopped the hounds, as Osbaldeston was to meet there next day." An excellent example.

There was a very hard day for hounds and horses on 11th December, when they whipped off after running for five hours, the last twenty minutes by moonlight. A day or two previous, he complains bitterly of a " confounded farmer " who gave him wrong information in order to prevent the field riding over the farm. This is the only mention made in the whole of the Diaries of any trouble with the farmers or yeomen.

" January 16th, 1819. Baxterley.—Twenty-three couples; Y. P. Found in Bentley Park, after one rattle round the covert, went to ground in the main earth. Drew Merevale Gorse and the Grendon woods blank. Went and bolted a fox out of a drain close to Grendon House; ran him by Warton, where he was headed, crossed the river, past Lord Grey's House, and killed him near Ratcliffe after thirty-five minutes without a check; a dog-fox. Rode Lupus and Skylark; Kit, Chicken; Jack, Doctor."

The Diary for this season ends here abruptly, but mentions that it was " a very good season, a great deal of hunting, and killed thirty-nine and a half brace of foxes."

THE PYTCHLEY COUNTRY

1820-21

ON taking the Pytchley country in 1820, Sir Bellingham went to live at Harleston, and was evidently determined to lose no time in making a start, his first day being 31st July, a date which in most countries would be quite impossible.

On July 31st at Lilford Wood; twenty-six couple of old hounds and twelve of young ones; found a "good breed of foxes," which they hunted for three hours and forty minutes, eventually killing one.

On August 4th at Brampton Wood; hounds changed from a fox on to a badger, which they killed, afterwards catching a cub in the same place.

"August 7th, Geddington Chase.—Thirty-five couples; found directly and ran for several hours, but the covert was so strong that I sent Will for seventeen couples of fresh hounds, by which means we killed, after running eight hours, a cub-fox; saw plenty of foxes. Rode Wellington; Will, Duke; Jack, Prince."

11th August.—After drawing Pipewell Wood and Carlton Purlieus, and only finding one old fox, he makes a note " to leave off hunting for a week or two, foxes not being so plentiful as I had imagined." Hounds were out again on the 26th, but he was justified in his remarks, as there were two blank days shortly after.

They had a hard day on 7th October, running in Stanion Purlieus from eleven till past six; five or six foxes on foot, but not one left the covert, and they did not get blood.

The other pack had hard luck next day on 9th October : " Found in Cranford Gorse, and ran very fast up to Grafton Park, through it, and to ground. Found in Geddington Chace; ran quick through Boughton Wood, Grafton Park, to Cranford Gorse; turned back and to ground under the cross-ridings in Grafton Park." Contrary to his usual custom he did not attempt to dig out either fox.

After a blank day at Rushton on 19th October, in the course of which he " found Weekley Hall Woods full of shooters," the hounds left Brigstock and went for a week to Fawsley Park, where Sir Charles Knightley then lived.

" October 30th. Sywell Wood.—Twenty-three couples; old pack. Found in Sywell Wood, where we had several foxes on foot; ran them about with a wretched scent for some time, till they all went over to Wilmore Park; got up to one at Orlingbury Wold, and ran him very quick a ring back to Sywell Wood, where we killed a cub dog-fox.

"Found again in Overstone Park; ran down to Billing Lings, Ecton, and brought him back dead beat into Overstone, where he went into a small sough under the road; left him for future sport; an hour and twenty-five minutes. Rode Yaffil and Skylark; Will, Charlotte; Jack, Emperor.

"October 31st. Sibbertoft. — Twenty-four couples; young pack. Found at Northorp; ran him quick up to Marston Wood, where he was headed, turned back; ran him all the line of Northorp Hills, sunk the valley, tried the earths, crossed the Harborough Road, and ran him into a drain close to the canal, but as it was Osbaldeston's country we left him. Found in a spinney close to the Woollies, three foxes; came away with one, the best pace, through the Woollies, by the Reservoir, over the turnpike road, by Cold Ashby, and up to Thurnby Grange without a check—twenty-seven minutes' best pace; there came to a long check; went on with him past Guilsborough up to Cottesbroke, where we got upon the line of another fox, and he beat us at last—a very fair day's sport. Rode Beeswax; Will, Cardinal; Jack, Duchess."

The cub-hunting thus finished with two good

days. Although the Diary calls October " the worst hunting month I ever recollect," sport does not seem to have been so bad.

Hunted thirty-five days, but only killed fifteen foxes.

"November 7th. Church Brampton.— Twenty-two couples; Y. P. Drew Cank blank; found in Wright's Gorse; went away very sharp past Ravensthorpe, and killed close to Coton— twenty-six minutes—a cub bitch-fox. Found a brace in the spinney close to Blackthorn; ran up to Holdenby, then turned to the right and came down to the corner of Harleston Park—fifteen minutes, best pace without a check; ran him through the park and pheasantry, and into the heath, where we had several foxes on foot. Rode Leopold and Weaver; Will, Shepherd; Jack, Rainbow.

"November 10th. Stanford Hall.—Twenty-two couples; young pack. Found in the first gorse, but the people, both foot and horse, halloed and disturbed the hounds so that they did not settle; however, we ran him nearly to Misterton, but the hounds were so flashy and wild we soon lost him. Drew Yelvertoft Field Side and Elkington Bottoms blank; found in Nethercote's Gorse; ran him beautifully over Naseby Field, and just as he had nearly reached the end some cursed greyhounds picked her up—a cub bitch-fox. Rode Skylark and Wellington; Will, Taffety; Jack, Runner.

FOX-HUNTING RECOLLECTIONS

"November 13th. Kelmarsh.—Twenty-five couples; old pack. Found three foxes by the Engine Pond; ran a fair pace past Hazelbeech, over a corner of Naseby Field, by Parson's Hill, over the Cottesbroke Vale, nearly to Brixworth; turned to the left over the turnpike road, past Lamport, and ran him to ground one field from Short Wood—one hour and ten minutes. Found again in Scotland Wood; went over Naseby Field, and along the brook in the bottom nearly to Thurnby; crossed over the turnpike road to Thurnby Grange; was there headed; went past Guilsborough Grange and down to Coton Plantation, where we were running into him when a fresh fox jumped up; up to Coton—an hour at a very good pace. Went on with the fresh fox up the valley to West Haddon; left it close on the right; after that we went over some magnificent country, but not knowing it sufficiently I cannot describe the places by name; however, it ended by our running into our fox at Watford, the hounds killing her in a sheet of water in front of the house—an old bitch-fox; an hour and twenty minutes from the time we changed at Coton. It was by far the best day's sport I ever saw—only five horses were up when we killed, all the others being stopped long before. Rode Hesperus and Weaver; Will, Cardinal; Jack, Emperor."

The Diary says that he got a fall at the first fence on 16th November, and saw nothing at all of a good run from Crick Osier Bed, past Long Buckby and Whilton, to Brockhall.

Very fair sport continues, hounds running every day; the following two seem about the best at this period:—

"November 28th. Clipston. — Twenty-one couples; old pack. Drew Marston Wood blank. Found at Hothorp; ran him very quick the line of hill; back again away past Sibbertoft, close to Nethercote's Gorse, over Naseby Field, and killed her at the Woollies—a cub bitch-fox; very nice forty-five minutes. Drew Scotland Wood blank. Found at the Engine Pond; went away to the Dales by Hazelbeach on to Pursers Hills, and back again, and kept ringing round with several foxes till near dark. Rode Beeswax and Weaver; Will, Gravenell; Jack, Lightning.

"November 29th. Glendon. — Twenty-two couples; young pack. Drew Glen Gorse, Rushton Spinney, Gaultney Wood, and found in Alder Wood; ran very fast through Gaultney Wood up to Brampton Wood, through it very quick, through Hermitage Wood down to Braybrook, and ran into him in one of those large fields near Arthingworth; fifty minutes—an old dog-fox; a very excellent run. Rode Yaffil and Leopold; Will, Sally; Jack, Shepherd."

His field appears to have been unruly at times. On the 1st of December at Kelmarsh their first fox was headed in every direction and chopped.

Later in the day "found in Rokeby Gorse, but the hounds were halloed so much and made so ungovernable by that and the field riding close upon them, that I stopped them." In spite of these difficulties they had a fair day's sport, and killed two foxes.

"December 7th. Thurnby Lane.—Twenty-two couples; O. P. Drew Stanford Hall blank. Tried an osier bed close to Welford, where we found, but the hounds were so close to him in coming away that he turned back, and the tail hounds caught him — an old dog-fox. Found in Nethercote's Gorse; went away very quick near to Marston Wood; turned to the right almost to Farndon, up to Marston Wood—very fast for forty minutes; we then came to slow hunting, and we finished by running him into a drain at Farndon; a very pretty run. Rode Skylark and Richmond; Will, Sally; Jack, Duchess.

"December 22nd. Arthingworth.—Twenty-four couples; B. P. Found in the gorse, and went away the best pace past Kelmarsh Earths, through Scotland Wood, on to Maidwell Dales, where we had two or three scents and got beat. Drew Nethercote's Gorse and Kelmarsh Spinnies blank. Found in Faxton Corner; went very fast to Short Wood, headed back, through the Corner, over Harrington Dales, Rothwell Field, by Thorp Underwood, through Scotland Wood, and killed, about three fields on the other side of it, a bitch-fox; an exceeding good run of fifty-nine minutes. Rode Thunderbolt and Banbury Horse; Will, Sledmere; Jack, Tilton. Hesperus went home early, lame.

"December 23rd. Badby. — Twenty-two couples; D. P. Found a brace immediately; went away quick over Fawsley Park; he then turned to the left near to Newnham, on to Dodford Wold, past it and into a drain close to the canal near Brockhall—a very pretty run for forty-five minutes. After some trouble, bolted him; ran him a terrible pace of ten minutes and killed him, a very old dog-fox. We were so long at the drain I did not draw again. Rode Wellington and Victory; Will, Gravenell; Jack, Rummer."

Frost then stopped hunting till 10th January, when, although "the grass land was a sheet of ice, and it was scarce possible to hunt," they succeeded in getting out.

The next day he was riding a new horse, Grimaldi, who refused every fence with him, and lost him a good gallop (he does not appear to have ridden him again), but in the afternoon they had "an exceeding fine run of one hour and seventeen minutes from Wilmore Park, first a ring to Hardwick, and back through the park, then away past Cransley, Thorpe, and Broughton, to ground at Pytchley Earths."

"January 22nd, 1821. Fox Hall.—B. P. Drew Faxton Corner, Mawsley Wood, Cransley blank. Found in Gibb Wood ; ran through Wilmore Park, and over to Sywell Wood; came away to Hardwick and up to Orlingbury, then to the right, and lost him at the back of Great Harrowden. Drew the Harrowden Gorses, as usual, blank. Found later in Hardwick Wood, and went at a capital pace past Hardwick and up to Great Doddington in twenty-four minutes ; he there got run by some cur dogs, and we hunted into the Gardens about Wellingbro' at dark. Rode Beeswax and Yaffil.

"January 26th. Charlton.—B. P. Found in Staverton Wood, and went away up to the village; there the fog was so thick, and the hounds turning short, flung the whole field, and after a great deal of scouring about the country, I with a few others succeeded in getting up just in time enough to see them kill their fox two fields from Dodfold Wold—an old bitch-fox ; one hour from the time we found. Found in Dodfold Wold; ran him up to the left of Badby Wood, over Knightley's Park, and to ground in one of the Fishpond Drains ; a very good day. Rode Wellington and Beanstalk.

"February 5th. Naseby.—B. P. Drew the Woollies, Hothorp, Nethercote's Gorse blank. Found at Engine Pond; ran him about a little time, and he went into a stable ; got him and turned him down below the house ; he ran about ten minutes and we caught him close to Harrington—a dog-fox that had been wired. Found in Arthingworth Gorse; went away very quick by Langborough, over the Turnpike road, then to the right nearly to Oxendon; turned again over the road, along the Braybrook Grounds, and up through Hermitage Wood—thirty-nine minutes' capital; ran him up on to Brampton Wood, brought him back over the Earths, and killed him in the Hermitage Wood—an old dog-fox; an exceeding good run. Rode Skylark and Leopold."

Soon after this the Diary ceases, and it is only mentioned that hunting continued four days a week until the end of the month. Sport appears to have been quite excellent throughout, and the Pytchley was what he had long wished for; but why Sir Bellingham left that splendid country after one brief season must for ever remain a mystery. Whatever the cause may have been, it was evidently not in order to retrench, as the following autumn of 1821 he was to be found Master of the Quorn, with his hunting establishment on a larger scale than ever.

THE QUORN

1821-23

SIR BELLINGHAM this season started cub-hunting on 6th August at Lee Wood; he appears to have been well off for hounds, as he twice brought out fifty couples in August.

Ground very hard and dry, but they made a good start, killing eleven foxes in the first nine days; on 5th September, although they did not kill, hounds had a good day's sport; after hunting two foxes in the morning at Swithland, found in a small gorse, and ran very fast by Woodhouse and Beaumanor to Swithland and back, " losing him when they got on the fallow—a good twenty-five minutes."

He says later on: " Dry and bad weather for hunting beyond what I ever recollect "; and again: " The hounds were running near eight hours under a burning sun " at Widmerpool. One day in October he appears to have enjoyed himself much, when hounds slipped away with a fox from Whittington Rough, and they ran by Thornton

Rough and Bagworth into Nailstone Whigs, changed foxes there, and ran by Odstone House back into Odstone Gorse to ground—" a very excellent run of an hour and a quarter ; no one got away but myself and Will."

Forty days' cub-hunting, and killed twenty-nine foxes.

The opening day was at Kirby Gate, 4th November, but did not do much, eventually killing a fox in Somerby Village.

" November 18th. Quenby. — Twenty - two couples ; D. P. Found in Coplow and killed ; went away with another by Tilton and Marefield, going for Owston, and killed — thirty-one minutes. Found at Baggrave ; ran two severe rings, then went away, and killed two fields from Ashby Pasture—one hour thirteen minutes; capital day's sport. Rode Peter and Toby.

" November 21st. Kettleby.— Twenty - two couples ; O. P. Found at Goodyear's Gorse ; went into Saxilby by Wartnaby Stonepits, up the hill to Grimston, then down into the vale; back to Dalby Wood, Grimston, Frisby, Rotherby, Brooksby, and Hoby, two fields from which we ran into him—two hours ten minutes; very good day. Rode Beeswax and Jury."

They had a good thing on 26th November. Found in Norton Gorse ; went away past Galby, and killed close to Billesdon—a very quick sixteen minutes. "I got a hard fall and was taken to Rolleston."

This fall kept him in till 3rd December, when they had a good gallop. After killing a fox in the morning at Barkby Holt, found at Scraptoft, went away by Keyham, Thurnby, Barkby Holt, Baggrave, Quenby Hall, and up to Newton Hill; there he was coursed by some cur dogs and lost; "a very good run of an hour and fifty minutes."

Three days later, finding at Foxton, went away by Peatling through Walton Holt nearly to Stanford Hall, where he was lost in a violent storm; "a very good run—straight nine miles in fifty minutes."

"December 10th. Loseby. — Twenty-one couples; O. P. Found in the Gorse and ran by Quenby, Hungarton, and into a drain at Baggrave. Drew Ashby Pasture and Cream Lodge blank. Found in Thorpe Trussells; went away over Burrow Hill, by Somerby, through Orton Park, Brook, Manton, and stopped the hounds at dark going for Beaumont Chase; a capital run of an hour and twenty-five minutes. Rode Peter and Norton."

Frost here intervened for ten days.

"December 23rd. Quenby. — Twenty-one couples; O. P. The ground so hard, there was not a soul out except Frank Needham of Hungarton. Found in Botany Bay; ran like the wind, by Billesdon, towards Galby, then to the left by Tilton, and killed him close to Loseby; thirty-five minutes very capital. Rode Peter.

"January 3rd, 1823. Beaumanor.—Twenty-nine couples; Y. P. Went out for exercise as the ground was very hard. Found in Macklin Wood; ran by the Outwoods, Holywell Hall, over Garendon Park by Shepsted, and killed close to Oakley Wood—a very good run of one hour and five minutes. Rode Leopold.

"January 7th. Oadby.—Twenty-one couples; O. P. Found in Glen Gorse; ran a sharp ring, and to ground at Stretton. Found again at Norton Gorse; ran fast to ground at Burton. Found again at Norton Spinney; ran very fast by Glen, and on for Houghton, where we lost—a bad foggy day. Rode Peter and Houghton.

"January 8th. Kibworth. — Twenty-four couples; Y. P. Found at Gumley; ran very fast up to Laughton Village, and killed. Found at Fleckney; ran a wide ring by Bruntingthorpe and lost. Found at Laughton Hill; ran ten minutes and killed. Went away with another fox by Walton Holt and Misterton, pointing for Stanford, and stopped the hounds at dark — a capital straight fast run of an hour and sixteen minutes. Rode Baron and Norton.

"January 31st. Braunston.—Twenty-nine couples; Y. P. Did not find till we got to Whetstone; ran a ring back to Whetstone and away down to Narborough, very fast for twenty minutes, but soon lost, as there was so much snow water on the ground. Drew Enderby blank. Rode Oculist and Freemason."

There appears to have been much snow and frost this season. After the 9th of January, excepting one or two days, there was no hunting for many weeks, and subsequently these notes were not resumed; but it is clear that after two apparently successful seasons with the Quorn, Sir Bellingham quitted Leicestershire for ever, though he continued as M.F.H. elsewhere for a few more years. Owing to some of the old diaries being incomplete it has been difficult to produce more than a general summary of what occurred, omitting mention of doubtful days and recording only periods of the best sport.

This, indeed, has been my constant aim throughout the pages of these rambling recollections, and from first to last I have been much inclined towards the maxim of those words on the old sundial:

"Let others tell of storms and showers,
I only mark the sunny hours."

INDEX

Ailesbury, Marquis of, 83.
Albrighton Hunt, The, 149, 160–162.
Andover, Viscount, 19, 146.
Antrobus, Sir Edmund, 89, 94.
Ashburton, Lord, 9.
Atherstone Hunt, The, 149, 151, 168–184.

Badminton, 17.
Badsworth Hunt, The, 149–150.
Beaufort, Duke of, 11–12, 14, 37, 56–61, 87.
Beaufort Hunt, The, 13–17.
Bedale Country, The, 128–148.
Bentinck, Lord Henry, 22, 24.
Bicester Hunt, The, 25, 124.
Bissett, Mr. Fenwick, 16–17.
Blankney Hunt, The, 22, 24.
Brontë, Charlotte, 128.
Brown, Mr. Gilpin, 140.
Burton, Dick, 81.
Burton Hunt, The, 22, 23, 32, 62, 79.

Carter, George, 81.
Chaplin, The Right Hon. Henry, 19, 23, 25, 33, 52.
Chapman, Bob, 15, 37, 38.
Chesham, Lord, 25, 124.
Cirencester, 37.
Compton, Mr. Henry, 64, 72.
Cotswold Hunt, The, 35, 45.
Cotswold Hunt, The North, 38, 41.

INDEX

Coventry, Lord, 38, 41.
Crimea, The, 2.

Davenport, M.P., Mr. Bromley, 15.
Day, John, 7.
De Crespigny, Sir Claude, 69–70.
Devon and Somerset Staghounds, The, 16.
Doneraile, Viscount, 23.
Drake, Mr., 30.

Ede, George, 18.
England, General Sir Richard, 3, 5.

Freeman, Frank, 137.
Fricker, Jack, 83–86, 99.
Fritham, 71, 76.
Foljambe, F. J. S., 24, 28.

Gilbert, of Lambs Corner, Mr., 49.
Goddard, Jack, 53, 67.
Graham, Sir Bellingham, 130, 149–199.
Graham, Lady, 123.

Hambledon Hunt, The, 6, 149, 152–153, 167.
Harborough Market, 1.
Harriers, 142–147.
Hawtin, Charley, 22, 23, 24, 33, 67, 70–71.
Hills, Tom, 36, 38.
Holland, Fred, 135.
Hurworth Country, The, 25, 101–124.
Hursley Hunt, The, 7.

Jockey Club, The, 19.

Kemble, Adelaide, 8–9.
Kemble, Fanny, 8–9.
Kingscote, Colonel, 15.

Leeds, The Duke of, 130, 135–136.
Leigh, Sir E. Chandos, 33, 34.

INDEX

Le Marchant, General Sir Gaspard, 5.
Little, Captain, 16.
Londesborough, Lord, 59, 65.
Long, Walter, 7, 59.
Lonsdale, Lord, 24, 116, 164.
Lovell of Hincheslea, Mr., 47, 48.

Mandeville, Alfred, 72, 73.
Milbank, Squire, 129–130.
Miles, Colonel, 15.
Mytton, John, 160, 161, 165.

Netheravon House, 83, 100.
Nevill, Mr., 7.
New Forest, The, 25, 46–78.
Newmarket, 20.
Nicoll, Will, 116.
"Nimrod," 101–109, 154, 157–158, 164–165.
Norton Conyers, 2, 123, 125–128, 135, 142–143, 149, 159.

Osbaldeston, Mr., 62, 141, 153, 159–160, 164, 183.
Osborne, John, 18.

Park, Mr. A., 122.
Paulet, Sir Henry, 59, 64.
Payne, George, 20, 21.
Pitt, Rev. Joseph, 43–45.
Poitou, 11, 12.
Powell, Colonel Martin, 59, 65.
Pytchley Hunt, The, 21, 62, 137, 149, 152–153, 160, 185–194.

Quorn Hunt, The, 15, 62, 79, 149, 153–160, 195–199.

Raby Hunt, The, 128, 137–142.
Rokeby, 141.
Rous, Admiral, 20.
Russell, Hon. Edward, 11.

Sandhurst, Royal Military College, 2.
Sartoris, Edward, 8–9.

INDEX

Sartoris, Mr. Edward, *see* Adelaide Kemble.
Shropshire Hunt, The, 149, 162–167.
Smith, Thomas Assheton, 79–81.
Somerset, The 14th Duke of, *see* Lord Algernon St. Maur.
Somerset, Q.C., Granville, 16, 17.
Somerset, Colonel Poulett, 14.
St. Maur, Lord Algernon, 59, 89, 94.
Sutton, Sir Richard, 15, 31.

Tailby, Mr., 142.
Tedworth Country, The, 79–100.
Travess, Charles, 39, 40.
Tredcroft, Edward, 6.
Tregonwell, Mr., 7.
Tubb, John, 8.

Vane-Tempest, Lord Henry, 122–123, 140.
Vyne Hunt, The, 7.

Warde, Mr. John, 50.
Warnford Court, 8.
Webb, Mr. Godfrey, 86–87.
Whyte-Melville, George, 1, 51, 159.
Wilkinson, Matthew, "Nimrod's" account of a hunt with, 101–109.
Wilkinson, Mr. T., 122.
Winchester, 6.
Wolf-hunting, 11, 12.
Wolverton, Lord, 51.
Wootton, Will, 143.
Worcester, Lord, 11, 14, 57.
Wyndham, Hon. Henry, 11.
Wyndham, Hon. Percy, 88, 94, 95.

Yorkshire Hound Show, 66.

Zetland, Lord, 137–142.